XMAS 05

Mom —

With love from Colombia
We have high expectations
for our next visit!

Love, Alexander,
Zara & Jennifer
(in order of Colombianess ☺)

The Taste of Colombia

The Taste of Colombia

Direction
BENJAMIN VILLEGAS

Edition
GLORIA MERCEDES DUQUE

Production
MASCHA KAUKA

Studio photography
HANS DÖRING

Texts
ANTONIO MONTAÑA

Villegas
editores

This book has been created, researched and published
in Colombia by,
© VILLEGAS EDITORES 1994
Avenida 82 No. 11 - 50, Interior 3
Telephone (57-1) 616 1788. Fax (57-1) 616 0020
Bogotá D.C., Colombia
e-mail: villedi@cable.net.co

www.villegaseditores.com

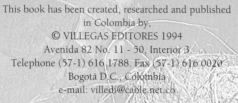

Design
BENJAMÍN VILLEGAS

Production coordinator
PILAR GÓMEZ

Art and reproduction
MERCEDES CEDEÑO, LORENA PINTO

Culinary research
ISABEL CORPAS DE POSADA

Additional photographs
HANS DÖRING
JEREMY HORNER
DIEGO MIGUEL GARCÉS
JOSÉ FERNANDO MACHADO

English translation
DENISE MICHELSEN

Revised and corrected
ANDREW ALEXANDER REID

Third edition
November 2001

ISBN
958-9138-98-5

The editor wishes to express special thanks to
CREDIBANCO and VISA COLOMBIA
for having sponsored the first edition of this book.

Photos on the first pages
Pages 2/3: Chicken and Oxtail Stew
Pages 4/5: Coffee
Pages 6/7: Rondown with dumplings
Pages 8/9: Cacao

Contents

Foreword

Getting to know the native food of a country is as rewarding experience as learning its language. When we try the dishes that come from a certain part of the world we not only learn about the people who live there but also share something of its past. The taste of a rich, exotic dish makes us part of its myths, migrations, adventures and resources. It enables us to enter into the imagination of its women when they added new products and recipes to their local cuisine, adapting it to climactic conditions, available utensils and the needs of the men who laboured under the intense heat of the tropics or the hard frosts and mists of the highlands.

This is not a book for culinary experts. It is, instead, a gift –as well as a challenge– to enthusiasts of cooking. It is a book for those who wish to share a similar adventure and experiment with the varied gastronomic possibilities which the land, history and local

Ajís *of avocado, herbs and egg*

traditions contributed to the flavour of Colombian food.

Its original inhabitants invented recipes, based on maize, cassava, roots, chili pepper, wild game and fish, that formed the foundation of local dishes which, with time, were perfected into a cuisine that satisfies the most refined palates. The Afro-American community contributed such ingredients as coconut and palm oil, and the cultivation of such fruits as the papaya, avocado, pineapple and mango. In their "palenques", rustic fortresses of palisades where they sought refuge from slavery, they grew foods which are the basis of our present-day cuisine. The Spanish, for their part, brought their table traditions, dishes also nourished by exotic elements, especially Muslim ones, that were quickly adapted to the conditions and taste of the creoles, a mane given to the freemen born in these lands.

Because of this varied racial and geographical background, it is difficult to speak of a single Colombian culinary tradition. "El Sabor de Colombia" takes this into account, and carefully presents the characteristics of each tradition, so that the reader will have the chance to choose those dishes that appeal to his tastes.

Those who wish to try out an exotic soup, like the "mondongo" (a native version of a Spanish original), the stew of Bogotá or a simple but delicious and fortifying potato consommé may do it without complications. Lovers of international cuisine, for their part, will find such recipes as the always exquisite lobster salad, rice with shrimps or other shellfish and pig's haunch, traditional Christmas dishes which are seasoned with well-known spices like black pepper, onion, cloves, garlic and laurel. And for those who are still able to permit themselves the luxury of eating a rich dessert, there are many varieties. Those with a fruit base, for example, like the "bocadillo" prepared with sifted guavas, blackberry sweet or stewed figs. Or the "arequipe" which deliciously combines the flavours of milk, sugar and cinnamon, ingredients that are found in any well-stocked kitchen.

This book is also a feast of contrasting flavours, textures and aromas. The simplicity of some of the meals which are presented here will delight those who love wholesome foods and those who understand that it is not necessary to recur to a fancy presentation or elaborate decoration to make a dish look

Rice with pepitoria

attractive. The rich colours of tropical fruits or fishes and seafood are, in themselves, sufficiently beautiful to please the eye and stimulate a pleasant conversation, ingredients which are as important to a good table as the food itself.

As the reader experiments with our recipes, he will become familiar with the abundance of the Colombian coasts, which have enriched the pleasures of dining with the fruits of its seas and gardens and its dishes based on rice, coconuts and root vegetables. So too with our coffee-growing regions, where the farmer who works from dawn to dusk has created a wholesome and nourishing diet of beans and maize cakes. Or that of Greater Cauca, whose centenary agrarian tradition has been enriched by the ingenuity of the Black and Indian women who worked in the kitchens of aristocratic landowners: fruit juices, the "empanada" or deep-fried meat pie, shell and sea fish, and pork. In the regions of Santander and La Guajira itinerant traders helped developed local dishes that please the palate and which our reader will also learn about. To say nothing of the remote and mysterious lands of the Orinoco and Amazon, which gave rise to such exotic recipes as the millenary cassava flour or smoked fish, products of a region where cooking oil is scarce.

We urge you to begin experimenting with the flavours of Colombia, and hope you will enjoy the feast which we offer here!

Ingredients used for making Hogao, Hogo *and* Guiso

Introduction

Geography explains flavors and colors. Therefore, a book striving to compile the cuisine of a country must start with a glance at the environment, its basic larder.

Colombia is a tropical country, and this implies much more than the term might suggest. Tropical isn't synonym with disarray, joyous riot, infectious music. It can be all of the above, but it also involves a mysterious factor: the climate.

Colombia is a tropical country. This means that days have the same length all year round. The daylight hours are always the same, something which doesn't happen north or south of the imaginary line which cuts the world in half. As the tropical zone presents a varying angle to the sun, there are no seasons, no winter, spring, summer or autumn to speak of. Changes in temperature in the tropics are related to altitude, for every 180 meters upwards, the temperature drops one degree. Thus, in a tropical country,

Desert of La Tatacoa, Huila

during the same day the traveler can experience the stifling heat of the lowlands, the temperate climate of the plateaus under an altitude of 1800 meters, the cold of the high plains and the harsh freeze of the high mountains of eternal snow.

In the tropics, winter and summer are measured in terms of wet and dry seasons; the former are known as winter and the latter as summer. Moreover, rainfall is intimately related to winds. In a tropical country humidity and rainfall levels are not uniform; they are closely related to orography, in other words to geographical factors. Along the Pacific coast, for example, Colombia possesses one of the rainiest zones in the world, while La Guajira, to the north, on the Caribbean, is the only desert on the entire American continent's Atlantic.

Due to all these geographic and climatic circumstances, there is not one Colombia, but many. And instead of one flavor and color, variety and abundance. Tropical Colombia can be an endless surprise. Geographers, nowadays of a much less tedious variety than those who taught us numbers, figures and colors on maps during our schooldays, often use the term microclimate. In a given region, it's not only one climate which holds sway. Higher or lower humidity, the presence or absence of winds and many other factors create substantial changes in the vegetation, fauna and customs of the local human communities. A country is generally divided into natural areas, in other words regions of similar orography and climatology. Which is valid within a geographical context, but in this case the purpose of division is to explain a form of culture: cooking. Therefore we must consider elements unrelated to nature, such as history, for instance, and consequently social sciences.

Nonetheless, for the purpose of this book, we have divided the country into eight cultural regions: the Caribbean coast and plains, forming a vast territory united in culture but not in landscape; the region of Santa Fe de Bogotá, the culinary history of which is tainted by what sociologists call "metropolitanism"; the Cundinamarca and Boyacá altiplano, a geographical environment determining a certain type of staple foods; the Cauca basin, a constant statement of *mestizo* culture and tastes; Antioquia and Viejo Caldas, where the table is laden with history and character; northern and southern

Santander and La Guajira; and Tolima Grande, another chapter on our voyage. The eighth region includes the Orinoco and Amazon.

Landscape creates regional identity. Behavior and preferences endow them with a different form of identity, culture, which is intimately linked to communications. Roads reduce distances: they allow for exchange and shared food habits. But there is a kind of communication other than physical, the verbal exchange of experience, the transfer of knowledge by education or oral tradition. Communities find identity and unity through culture, in other words, they assert themselves through likes and dislikes. Communications integrate a region and end up defining its character.

A regional culture is the sum and consequence of such diverse factors as history, climate and a living and variable element which combines landscape, manners and common aspirations. And it is means of communication which keep the separate geographic regions connected to the great whole that constitutes a culture.

Landscape, in the sense of natural environment, is the primary source of nourishment, but food preferences and culinary techniques are a matter of culture. Regional products logically prevail in a given area, but in a city consumer trends and the existence of markets offering fare from all over the

Fruit from the jungle, Quibdo, Chocó

Vegetables in Corabastos market

country allow for variety. In turn, such a palatable repertoire will soon spread to the surrounding region. These changes are historical, in other words cultural. Popular Colombian cuisine has been defined, in a manner which is correct from the historical perspective, as *criollo*. *Criollo*, however, doesn't mean native, autochthonous, grass-roots, but the product of a mixture. Indeed, every cuisine, as every culture, is the result of a combination of elements coming from different places.

Jungle in the Magdalena Medio, Santander

The term *criollo* was introduced well into the eighteenth century, derived from the word *créole*, a Haitian hodgepodge dialect of French and African idioms. The term soon defined everything which resulted from the blend of European and American. Thus the son of a Spaniard born in America was *criollo*, and henceforth the combination of any elements from the two continents. The sauce made with onion brought by the Spaniards and the native tomato is called *criollo*. The combination of garlic and corn in the Andean *mazamorra* is also *criollo*.

And, in the culinary field, we call *criollización* the process of cultural miscegenation, the contribution of techniques and flavors to a native cuisine creating a new one. A good example is *arepa de huevo*. This favorite Caribbean tidbit is of Tunisian origin: the *brick bil lham*. The adaptation begins when the local cook uses products which, at a pinch, can replace the original ones, until obtaining a different but satisfactory result. The *brick bil lham* reappeared on the Colombian coast with a new flavor, texture and name. In unmistakable Spanish fashion, it was called *empanada*, and originally brought by a group of Syrian immigrants in 1902. The first generation concocted the *brick bil lham* for a limited public, but its fame spread quickly, and by the second generation the name and origin had been forgotten. It was already called *empanada de huevo* in Cartagena or *arepa de huevo* in the rest of the country. This is just one of many culinary examples of cultural *criollización*. Nobody today would deny that food is an essential part of national expression; that its presence in history is, as any work of man, culture: a sum of activities achieved by people in order to transform the environment into something amenable and personal. As any cultural form, such as language for instance, culinary customs change, adapt and undergo influences when confronted with alien manifestations.

There is no culture, just as there is no living organism, which isn't in constant change. When all is said and done, culture is what life is about.

Caribbean Coast and Plains

Layers of quaternary sediment swept away by water over centuries. Rock deposits patiently accumulated during thousands of years. Here and there, a few elevations bring us back to the tertiary period, when tremendous cataclysms lifted or sunk entire territories, giving origin to the Sierra Nevada de Santa Marta and the vast plains of Cesar and La Guajira.

In the midst of the Caribbean plains, far from the sea, four great Colombian rivers meet: the Magdalena, Cauca, San Jorge and Cesar form an inner delta which, during the rains, fill the basin and flood enormous areas only to leave parched desolation in the dry season. Six months of the year the inhabitant of the *Mojana* lives on dry land, and the other six months on water. On the same soil, he's a fisherman during the flood season and a cattle rancher and farmer when the waters subside. His culture is amphibious.

Here, many centuries ago, before the Spanish conquest, a native civilization, the Chimila, managed thanks to inventiveness and effort to

Houses in Pasacaballos, Bolívar

overcome these geographical conditions. They built over hundreds of kilometers a drainage system that made agriculture possible during the flood season and fish and crab farming during the drought.

Traces of this great system are still visible today in aerial photographs. The land was shaped somewhat into a fishbone pattern, with alternating channels for sowing and draining. This colossal engineering feat, that we still envy six centuries after the disappearance of the civilization which created it, succeeded in solving problems that we have not managed to cope with to this day.

Around four hundred years B.C, the Indians already cooked their food in earthenware pots. We owe this knowledge to archaeologist Gerard Reichel Dolmatoff, who found in Puerto Hormiga, near the Canal del Dique, midway between Barranquilla and Cartagena, the most ancient American ceramics we know of. Such a "revolution" meant nothing less than the step from roast to ragout.

We know little about this indigenous group, and a lot at the same time. Cultures are not silent

Fisherman of Manaure, La Guajira

Sinú river, Córdoba

when they leave traces behind. We do not know where the group came from, although certainly from the south. But the mastery of earthenware techniques proved that its culture was advanced. Along with ceramic fragments were found pierced conch spirals, fishbones, turtle shells hammered open with stones, and remains of small mammals. These vestiges were discovered in a place where the community deposited its wastes, which indicates that it had settled there over a long period and lived of agriculture. It planted corn and, without doubt, used wild cassava originating from the Amazon.

The inhabitants of Puerto Hormiga were not savages. Selecting clays and blending them with corrosives and fats, which made them fit for firing and of lasting use, proves not only intelligence but also experience, the result of failure and success: apprenticeship. In other words, civilization.

The *Mojana* region, the interior delta, belongs culturally to the Caribbean coast. Its music, ethnic roots and very language are the same. Generally, local people eat smoked or dried fish. At low water,

fish are trapped in pools and caught effortlessly. Such is the fare during winter, when floods make fishing more difficult and fresh fish can be sold at a higher price. Rice is more common in the local diet than on the coast. It replaces cassava, yam and sweet potato, crops vulnerable to floods.

In 1500, the inhabitants of the Caribbean coast are hunters and pickers. They feed on roots and a variety of wild fruit, deer and large rodents are abundant. They are also fishermen, and in some regions actually farm fish, crabs and molluscs. As a dietary supplement, they consume insects and reptiles, or their eggs. To this day turtle and iguana eggs are part of the popular diet.

The Spaniards land in a region populated by fishermen, who trade fish for agricultural products with another, more advanced, group: the Tayrona. The latter cultivate their crops on terraces embracing mountain curves. Not only are the inhabitants of the Sierra Nevada de Santa Marta engineers but also skilful potters and magnificent goldsmiths. Of their architecture remain the paved roads and stone walls bordering their farmlands, and the labyrinth of their village streets. The tourist frequently stumbles upon mortars where they ground corn, material witnesses to an ancient way of life. Although we cannot be sure, it is probable that they used the flour to bake breads similar to *arepas,* to thicken vegetable broths, and that they toasted corn grains, as their descendants still do. Chroniclers also mention the fruit that Indians offered the strange visitors, before the latter discovered the magnificent gold jewelry they wore.

The Spanish wage a war of annihilation, yet their victory turns out to be Pyhrric. Within a few months, the newcomers will suffer from a hunger of savage proportions; everything in their new environment is unfamiliar, and therefore hostile.

The first enemy is the strange nature that surrounds them, and the second their own nature, which is weak. They are loaded with gold but can't buy anything with it. When their scarce supplies run out, their only recourse is to raid villages. Battles against the natives have the main objective of *rancheo,* or obtaining provisions.

The Spaniards establish settlements as bases to "discover lands", and their ships must then bring more pigs and chickens than troops of fighting men. Sacks of flour last as long as "an amen in the face of so much accumulated hunger".

The battle of the stomach is the first to be lost. After accepting defeat, the Spaniards settle for a compromise truce, learn to eat corn, cassava and other roots and quench their thirst with fruits,

Fishermen weaving their nets. Taganga, Magdalena

Fisherman in Parque Tairona, Magdalena

Ají picker, San Jacinto, Bolívar

described by soldier and poet Don Juan de Castellanos as "possessing the taste of all the vanilla in the world". From Santa Marta, expeditions penetrate inland. As they get further away from base and enter the unknown, the conquistadors depend more on themselves than on supply lines. The New World is filled with riches, but proves a desert for the empty belly. Worse still, food is so scarce that Gaspar Nuñez Cabeza de Vaca, after thirteen shipwrecks, confesses that to survive it was necessary to single out for eating among his companions "the one who was going to die soonest".

Game is few and far between. The tropical forest is rich in species of flora and fauna, but poor in individual specimens. Anyway, gunpowder becomes so scarce that it is reserved for battle. With only a few skilled bowmen available, they have to rely on the natives' marksmanship, which mysteriously misaims when the prey is to feed a Spaniard.

Transporting milk in Calamar, Antioquia

What did the Spanish find to eat that they were already familiar with? The list is short: plantains that they cultivated in the Canary Islands, and coconuts, the flesh and milk of which they had tasted. They knew nothing of all the rest: yam, sweet potatoes, corn, beans, potatoes, *malanga*, pineapple, and an endless list of other products. For this reason, the later conquistadors, in the mid-sixteenth century, arrive with their pockets full of seeds. Thanks to this foresight, oranges, lemons and tangerines, that the Arabs had brought to Spain, came to grow in America; and rice sprouted in the flooded lands, rice that the Mahommedans had taken first to Sicily and then to Spain. And the newly-introduced eggplants soon grew alongside the native squash.

In five hundred years of history, three cities in the Caribbean region relayed each other as centers of cultural expansion: Santa Marta was the

Fruit stall. Cartagena, Bolívar

base for territorial conquest during the 16th century and the economic machine for much of the 19th and early 20th centuries; Cartagena the great bastion and port during the Colonial and Republican eras and finally Barranquilla, born in the 20th century.

In ports, goods are disembarked, inevitably along with people driven by varying motives. Cartagena replaced Santa Marta as the center and point of departure of settlers, for a simple reason. A hundred years after the conquest began, other newcomers thirsting for gold and power appeared on the coast, agents of the French or English empires in the guise of pirates. And Cartagena is a defendable position, unlike Santa Marta. Its walled enclosure follows the outlines of swamps, channels and bogs. It is practically a lake city. The walls not only defend homes but also warehouses. Few men are needed to protect it, a safe, or at best less dangerous place for merchants and craftsmen.

In the mid-sixteenthth century, large groups of African slaves arrive in Cartagena, to replace the indigenous labor force decimated by disease, overwork and hunger. To reduce the extremely high mortality that the overcrowded voyage, without water or food, causes among Negroes, the Portuguese, and then Spaniards and English, load coconuts on the slave ships. Coconuts provide a natural package of water, protein and fat. Those left-over by dead human cargo are thrown into the Caribbean once harbour is in sight, and palm trees spring up along the coast.

Weighing fish. Rosario Islands, Bolívar

If the Spanish arrived with their pigs, milking cows, goats and seeds, the Negroes arrive with their misery, wisdom, coconuts, sesame and the knowledge and skills needed in a tropical environment. They are accustomed to living in similar habitats. They know that birds never eat the wrong fruit and that mushrooms of a bright red color are full of poisonous treachery. They eat sprouts and roots rejected by the Spaniards. They quickly discover fruit which yield oil, unlike the white man who persists in planting olive trees which grow but never yield.

Often, the Negroes flee from the white man's harsh treatment and found settlements deep in the jungle, the *palenques,* where they plant papayas, pineapples, avocados, dry-land rice, cassava… Far from masters and missionaries, they re-create their music and return to their customs. They speak their own languages and eat foods combining African and American flavors. *Carimañola,* the name of a popular and filling dish, is an African word which, like many others referring to foods and objects, became a regional colloquialism.

Cartagena, a city fortified at enormous expense, would come to symbolize the presence of Spain in the New World. Here landed the viceroys and officials. Battles were waged against the French, the English, the Dutch, against pirates and eventually troops from Spain. It was in Cartagena that the Holy Court of the Inquisition was established, with judges from the Dominican order. Convents were constructed by Jesuits,

Franciscans, Augustinians, and nuns of the Carmelite, St. Clare and Tertiary orders. Traders from Spain, and some from France and Italy, also set up shop. In the 16th century, Cartagena is a tropical version of the Tower of Babel. In the 18th century, ships arrive loaded with hoes, horses and cattle, everything that can't be found in America, and luxuries such as wine, olives, and olive oil. Such are the simple extravagances of people like *El Sabio* Mutis, the leader of the Botanical Expedition, who bequeaths to his nephew in his will these priceless treasures: a supply of olives, dried figs, almonds and two casks of olive oil.

In the early 19th century, after Independence, the streets of Cartagena smell of palm oil that the poor, the freed Negroes, *zambos* and *mestizos* cook with, and of the lard used by the rich, and on Sundays of coconut oil, sizzling at the bottom of the pan, the *titoté,* where rice will be fried. Store counters will already be displaying the *bollolimpio* to take to the beach as a side dish for fried

swordfish or fish stew. Cartagena filled with taverns whose thick-boarded tables served Valencia-style rice dishes, with *achiote* or *unoto* oils instead of saffron, rice perfumed by the sea and *chipi-chipi* stew. And as round-off, Caribbean rums and fruit brought by Negresses on platters balanced on their heads: papayas, pineapple, green mangos, watermelons red and juicy, *madroños* ripe and sweet, from the *palenque* orchards.

For a while, in the early 20th century, Santa Marta reasserts its regional leadership. It's the banana boom era. Rairoads, irrigation and transport sytems are built. Ships arrive laden with canned goods for the foreign employees of the banana companies and leave loaded with bananas. Foreigners aren't fond of the local food, until a wife discovers that ginger grows wild in the mountains, and turmeric, introduced by God knows who, known locally as *palo amarillo.*

In the first decades of the century, one sole province of the Caribbean coast, Bolívar, occupies

❧

Street food vendors. Cartagena, Bolívar

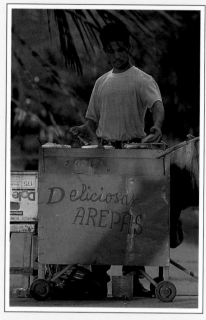

Native picking coconuts in San Andrés   *Red snappers from San Andres Island*   *Selling arepas on the beaches of Tolú, Sucre*

more territory than France, and the smallest, Atlántico, is the size of Holland. Wars drive thousands of men from their land, and condemn them to exile. Three great waves of immigrants, at three different periods, arrive on the coast of Colombia, and settle on its territory. They are not farmers, but even if they were, the geographical conditions are so different that their experience would be useless. Each group keeps its diet and customs, while at the same time adapting and modifing them. Native ingredients replace the original ones. Food of Arab, German and Italian origin spreads, while simultaneously acquiring a *criollo* touch. Pasta becomes part of the daily diet. Sausages become popular. Names of Arab foods are easier to pronounce: *sinuano* lentils, *negrito* rice, *indios*. The Chinese plant vegetables, and their vegetarian *empanada* ends up considered a native dish.

Barranquilla replaced Cartagena as cultural center in the first years of the century, when its sea harbor opened up to river navigation and the

Magdalena was able to handle all imports and exports. Blocked since 1870, the Canal del Dique, which linked Cartagena with the Magdalena river, no longer afforded passage to river boats bringing the products of half of Colombia to foreign markets. Barranquilla substituted Cartagena as the major port, and, in 1900, thanks to local immigration seeking work, its population reaches the same level. Table habits change. Restaurants open up, offering international food, and the recipes adapt to *criollo* taste in private homes.

The Caribbean plain is perhaps the area of Colombia which offers the greatest number of examples of *criollización*. And the reason is simple. Its coast faces an inner sea: the Caribbean, "the routes of which", *Libertador* Simón Bolívar used to say, "open out to the world".

Fruit platter

The presence of African culture on the American continent explains the use of coconut in a wide and varied number of typical dishes from the Caribbean plains. Coconut is used in soups, desserts, fish stews and, as in this case, to prepare delicious chicken in coconut milk.

Enyucado, *a cassava pastry*

Caribbean crabs, crammed with delicate meat, are famous among gourmets. Their texture is comparable to the finest species from the Southern Seas. Once the crab is cooked, the claws are removed and pounded gently to crack the shell open and reveal the flesh beneath. The sauce is up to you.

Stuffed squid

Crab claws in vinaigrette sauce

Sancocho de pescado, *like many other Colombian dishes, is a variation on the Spanish* cocido *theme. Basic preparation is the same, but different elements such as tropical fish, plantains, cassava, yams and the superlative coconut milk give a Caribbean touch to the dish.*

Rice with shrimp, Rice with chipi-chipi

Fish stew

Patacón pisao, or squashed and fried plantain slices, is an inseparable companion to food on the Caribbean coast. "It has the color of gold and the consistency of a crab shell. When one bites into it, the crisp surface and the pulp within melt in the mouth. I believe it should be called American bread", said a French traveller in 1820. True words to this day.

Ingredients for Oyster cocktail

Squashed and fried plantain

Arepa de huevo *is the native adaptation of a dish of Tunisian origin, which appeared in the early 20th century, after the arrival of a group of Arab immigrants on Colombia's Caribbean coast. Nowadays, most famed are those made in Luruaco, a village between Barranquilla and Cartagena.*

Rice with coconut

Arepa de huevo *and cassava balls stuffed with*

Rondown

Rondón

8 portions

2 lb (1 kg) of conch meat
salt and pepper to taste
1 lb (500 g) of salt pork, cut into
  small pieces
8 cups (64 fl oz / 2 l) of coconut milk
2 green plantains, peeled and sliced
1 lb (500 g) of cassava, peeled and
  cut into pieces
1 lb (500 g) of yam
1/2 lb (250 g) of sweet potatoes,
  peeled and diced
1/2 lb (250 g) of breadfruit, peeled
  and cut into chunks
24 dumplings
2 tablespoons of fresh basil and
  oregano, finely chopped

To prepare the dumplings:

1 lb (500 g) of flour
1/2 cup (4 fl oz/125 ml) of coconut milk
1/2 tablespoon of salt

*M*ix the flour, the coconut milk and
the salt, forming a soft dough. Set aside
for 15 minutes.
❧ With wet hands, roll into small rolls.
Cut them in pieces and set aside.

To prepare the *rondón:*

❧ Pound the conch meat to make it
tender. Simmer in a little water with
salt and pepper for ten minutes. Cut
into small pieces.
❧ Cook the salt pork in water for 15
minutes to remove the salt.
❧ Put the conch meat and the pork to
cook in the coconut milk.
❧ After 15 minutes add the plantains,
the cassava, the yam, and the sweet
potatoes. When they become soft,
about 25 minutes later approximately,
add the breadfruit, the dumplings and
the salt and pepper. Simmer gently for
20 minutes more. Add the herbs five
minutes before serving.

Coconut milk

Leche de coco

*T*ake a large coconut and open a
small hole. Extract the water from the
coconut, then break it open. Grate the
coconut meat.
❧ In order to extract the first milk place
the grated coconut on top of a clean
kitchen towel, or in a colander. Add
two cups of hot water and press. The
first milk will be thick.
❧ To obtain the second milk, add, to
the same gratings, two more cups of hot
water. Press the pulp again extracting
the milk. The second milk will be
lighter.

Conch rissoles

Albóndigas de caracol

8 portions

2 lb (1 kg) conch meat
2 green peppers, finely chopped
2 onions, finely chopped
3 garlic cloves, chopped
3/4 cup (6 oz) breadcrumbs
1/4 lb (250 g) of potatoes, peeled and
    cooked
2 eggs, beaten
2 sweet ajíes, finely chopped
2 hot ajíes, chopped
1 tablespoon coriander, finely chopped
salt and pepper to taste
oil

*P*ound the conch meat well, to make it tender and cook in water with salt for one hour.
❧ Grind the conch meat and combine with the green peppers, the onion, the garlic, the breadcrumbs and the potatoes. Add the eggs, the *ajíes,* the coriander and the salt and pepper.
❧ Mix together well. Shape balls about the size of an egg from the mixture. Fry in hot oil for 15 minutes until they are golden.

Fried mojarra

Mojarra frita

8 portions

16 medium mojarras
salt
lemon
oil

*C*ut the *mojarras* open and clean them. Season with salt and lemon.
❧ Fry them in abundant, very hot oil for 15 minutes. Lower the heat and continue frying until golden on both sides.

Bollolimpio

8 portions

3 lb (1.5 kg) of corn grains
salt
large corn husks
string

*P*lace the corn to soak overnight, removing any impurities.
❧ Throw out the water and cook the corn in fresh water for 30 minutes. Allow to cool.
❧ Drain the water, grind the corn and knead into a smooth dough.
❧ Wash the corn leaves and place three tablespoons of the corn dough on each leaf. Cover with a second leaf and wrap, folding the edges. Secure with the string.
❧ Cook in salted boiling water for 30 minutes.

Fried catfish

Bagre frito

8 portions

4 lb (2 kg) of catfish, cut into slices
4 tablespoons of lemon juice
salt and pepper to taste
4 eggs
4 tablespoons of wheat flour
2 tablespoons of parsley, finely chopped
oil

Season the fish slices with the lemon juice, the salt and the pepper and allow to marinate for one hour.
❧ Beat the eggs, the flour and the parsley, adding a bit of salt and pepper.
❧ Dip the fish slices in this batter and fry in very hot oil until they are golden on both sides.

Boronia

8 portions

2 ripe plantains, peeled and cut into pieces
2 lb (1 kg) eggplant, peeled and cut into small pieces
5 oz (150 g) of white cheese, grated
2 red onions, finely chopped
2 cloves garlic, chopped
oil
salt and pepper to taste

Cook the plantain in water for 30 minutes until it is quite soft.
❧ Fry the eggplants in oil for five minutes
❧ Mix the plantain and the eggplant and mash them with a wooden spoon. Add the cheese, the onion, the garlic and the salt and pepper. Stir vigorously.
❧ Sauté in three tablespoons of oil for five minutes, stirring constantly.

Fruit platter

Platón con frutas

Nothing creates a better impression of a region's culinary possibilities than its fruits. On the Atlantic coast of Colombia mother nature truly outdid herself. What abundance, what colors, what shapes, what aromas… what tastes! It is difficult indeed to make one's choice from the platter of melons, papayas, mameys, mangos, coconuts, lemons, bananas and watermelons. Yet the decision becomes even more difficult when the culinary talent of *Costeño* women transforms these fruits into jams, jellies, desserts and puddings, ices and juices.

Chicken in coconut

Gallina al coco

8 portions

1 chicken
4 cups (32 fl oz/1 l) of coconut
  milk (see page 44)
2 red onions, chopped
3 garlic cloves, chopped
1 red pepper, diced
4 sweet ajíes, diced
1/2 teaspoon of fragrant pepper
1 teaspoon of cumin
salt to taste

𝒫ut the chicken, cut into serving
pieces, in a pot along with three cups of
coconut milk. Add the onion, the garlic,
the red pepper, the *ajíes,* the pepper,
cumin and salt. Cook over medium
heat for one-and-a-half hours
approximately, until the chicken is
tender.
❧ Add the remaining cup of coconut
milk, stirring frequently to avoid
curdling.

Cassava cake

Enyucado

1 lb (500 g) of white cheese
1 large coconut
3 lb (1. 5 kg) of peeled cassava
1 cup (8 oz/250 g) of sugar
1 teaspoon of anise seeds, crushed
1 cup (8 fl oz/250 ml) of milk
4 tablespoons (2 oz/ 60 g) of butter
butter for greasing the pan

𝒢rate into a bowl, one on top of the
other, the cheese, the coconut, and the
cassava, and add the sugar, the crushed
anise seeds, the milk and the melted
butter.
❧ Mix all the ingredients together well
until obtaining a smooth dough. Set
aside for one hour.
❧ Place the dough in a greased pan and
put into an oven preheated to 300°F for
one hour.

Crab claws

Muelas de cangrejo

8 portions

40 sea crab claws
4 lemons
1/4 cup (2 fl oz/60 ml) vinegar
1 red onion, finely chopped
4 garlic cloves, chopped
1 seeded tomato, diced
salt and pepper to taste
4 sweet ajíes
1 tablespoon of parsley finely chopped
1/3 cup olive oil

𝒮immer the crab claws in a bit of
water during 30 minutes. Discard the
water.
❧ Mix the lemon, the vinegar, the
onion, the garlic, the tomato. Season
with salt and pepper. Add the *ajíes,* the
parsley and the oil. Marinate the crab
claws in this mixture during one hour.

Stuffed squid
Calamares rellenos

8 portions

3 lb (1.5 kg) of medium sized squid
4 oz (125 g) of butter
1/2 lb (250 g) of red onions, chopped
4 garlic cloves, chopped
1 green pepper, finely chopped
2 cups (1 lb/500 g) of cooked rice
2 hard boiled eggs, chopped
1 teaspoon of thyme
salt and pepper to taste
1/4 cup tomato purée
1/4 cup (2 oz/50 ml) cream
1 cup (8 fl oz/250 ml) milk
1/2 cup (2 oz/60g) breadcrumbs

Clean the squid, removing the skin and separating the tentacles. Set aside.
❧ Sauté in half the butter the separated tentacles, the onion, the garlic, the green pepper, the rice, the eggs, the thyme, and the salt and pepper. Add half of the tomato purée, and a bit of the cream. Stir well.

❧ Use this mixture to stuff the squid, and place them face up in a pan.
❧ Mix the rest of the butter, the remaining tomato purée, the cream and the milk. Cook over low heat, adding salt and pepper to taste until obtaining a thick sauce. Pour this over the squid, sprinkle with the breadcrumbs and place in an oven preheated to 300°F for 20 minutes.

Oyster cocktail
Coctel de ostras

8 portions

1 lb (500 g) of shucked oysters in their juice
1 tablespoon of white vinegar fermented with garlic
4 tablespoons of lemon juice
ají to taste
1/2 red onion finely chopped
1/2 cup (4 oz/125 g) tomato purée
salt and pepper to taste

Mix the vinegar, the lemon juice, the ají, the onion and tomato purée. Season with the salt and pepper.
❧ Add the oysters in their juice to this mix, serve chilled.

Fish stew

Sancocho de pescado

8 portions

4 lb (2 kg) of shad, cut into thick slices
salt and pepper to taste
2 lemons
oil
1 shad fish head
4 ripe plantains
10 cups (80 fl oz/2 1/2 l) water
2 lb (1 kg) of cassava, peeled and cut into
  pieces
2 lb (1 kg) of yam, peeled and cut into
  pieces
1/2 cup guiso (see page 50)
3 cups (24 fl oz/750 ml) of
  coconut milk (see page 44)
1 teaspoon fresh thyme

*R*ub the slices with the salt, pepper
and lemon juice. Fry the slices in
abundant oil during three minutes.
Remove and place on absorbent paper
to drain.

❧ Wash the shad fish head and fry in
the oil for two minutes.
❧ Wash the ripe plantains leaving their
peel intact, just cutting off the ends.
Place the plantains to cook in water
with the fish head, the cassava, the yam
and the *guiso*. Cook high for 20
minutes.
❧ Remove the ripe plantains from the
water, adding the coconut milk and
cook at medium temperature for ten
minutes. Stir frequently to avoid
curdling.
❧ Remove the fish head, adding salt
pepper and thyme to the broth. Add the
fish slices cooking low for another ten
minutes, without stirring.
❧ Remove the fish carefully and place
along with the other ingredients on a
platter. Peel the plantain now, cut it
into chunks and add it to the platter.
Drench the platter with the *guiso*.
❧ Strain the broth and serve separately.

Squashed and fried plantain

Patacón pisao

8 portions

4 green plantains
oil
salt
ají

*P*eel the plantains and cut into five-
centimeter slices. Fry them for five
minutes in abundant oil not too hot.
Remove and drain. Pound them flat.
❧ Dip the squashed slices in water
mixed with salt and *ají*. Fry them again
in very hot oil until golden.

Rice with shrimp

Arroz con camarones

8 portions

1 1/2 lb (750 g) of fresh shrimp
1 lb (500 g) of rice
1 cup guiso (see on same page)
5 cups (40 fl oz/1.25 l) of water
salt and pepper to taste

Wash the shrimp in fresh water. Cook them in five cups boiling water to which salt has been added for three minutes. Remove and reserve the water in which they were cooking.
❧ Peel the shrimp and remove their heads. Grind the heads in a mortar and mix them in the water.
❧ In the pot where the rice is to be prepared heat the *guiso,* add the rice, salt and pepper. Sauté during five minutes.
❧ Add the water in which the ground heads were mixed and cook over medium heat for 20 minutes, until the rice begins to dry.
❧ Add the shrimp and stir. Cover the pot and cook low for another 20 minutes.
❧ The rice should be moist.

Rice with chipi-chipi

Arroz con chipi-chipi

8 portions

2 lb (1 kg) of chipi-chipi shellfish, in their
*   shells*
5 cups (40 fl oz/1.25 l) water
1 cup guiso
1 lb (500 g) of rice
salt and pepper to taste

Wash the *chipi-chipi* in fresh water then cook in five cups of boiling water in a covered pot for ten minutes. The shells should open. Reserve the cooking water and strain it.
❧ Remove the *chipi-chipi* from their shells, discarding any which fail to open.
❧ In the same pot where the rice will be cooked, heat the *guiso.* Add the rice, the salt and pepper and sauté for ten minutes.
❧ Add the broth where the *chipi-chipi* was boiled and continue cooking over medium heat for 20 minutes more, or until the rice begins to dry.
❧ Add the *chipi-chipi* and stir. Cover the pot and cook low for 20 minutes more.
❧ The rice should be moist.

Guiso

2 red onions, finely chopped
6 stalks of green onion, chopped
4 ripe tomatoes, peeled and chopped
8 sweet ajíes, chopped
2 garlic cloves, chopped
1 tablespoon vinegar
1 tablespoon annatto
salt and pepper to taste
1/4 cup (2 oz/50 ml) oil

Mix the onion, the green onion, the tomatoes, the *ajíes,* the garlic and the vinegar. Add the annatto, the salt and the pepper. Sauté in hot oil over medium heat during 15 minutes.

Arepa de huevo

8 portions

1 lb (500 g) of yellow corn grains
salt
oil
8 eggs

*S*oak the corn overnight, eliminating any impurities.
❧ Throw away the water and cook the corn in fresh water for 30 minutes. Allow to cool.
❧ Drain the water, grind the corn and knead it with a little salt until obtaining a smooth dough.
❧ Make balls out of the dough, and on top of a damp dishcloth, or greased plantain leaf, flatten them out. The *arepas* should be half-a-centimeter thick and eight centimeters in diameter.
❧ Place one by one in abundant, very hot oil for three minutes until they rise and thicken.
❧ Remove them from the oil, drain. Open a small slit in the side. Slip a raw egg mixed with a teaspoon of salted water into the middle of the *arepa*.
❧ Seal the slit with a little fresh dough. Return the *arepas* to the hot oil and fry until golden.

Cassava balls stuffed with pork

Carimañolas

1 lb (500 g) pork
salt and pepper
1 1/2 lb (750 g) of cooked cassava
1/2 cup guiso (see page 50)
oil

*C*ook the pork in one cup of water, adding salt and pepper, for 45 minutes.
❧ Grind the cassava, adding salt and kneading until obtaining a smooth dough.
❧ Grind the cooked pork, add the *guiso* and mix together well.
❧ Make egg-shaped balls of dough with your hands. Press a hole into them with your thumb. Fill the cavity with the meat mixture.
❧ Close the hole, sealing it with dough. Fry in very hot oil until golden.

Rice with coconut milk

Arroz con coco

8 portions

6 cups (48 fl oz/1. 5 l) coconut
*   milk (see page 44)*
salt to taste
1 tablespooon sugar
1 lb (500 g) of rice

*B*oil the coconut milk until it is reduced by half. Add the salt, the sugar, the rice and stir.
❧ Cook for 20 minutes over medium heat, until the rice begins to dry. Cover the pot and cook low for another 20 minutes.

Following page: Ajiaco santafereño

Santa Fe de Bogotá

Truly, *Santafereño* food is subject to an unusual phenomenon: history confers it variety, but by tradition it is monothematic and austere.

Santa Fe, capital of the Viceroyalty of Nueva Granada, was founded in 1537 by Gonzalo Jiménez de Quesada on a plateau 2,600 meters above sea level, sheltered by the peaks of the Eastern Cordillera. After crossing jungles dark even in daytime and ridges swept by icy winds, the sight of green pastures reminiscent of fertile Granada filled Quesada with joy: "Oh, good land, land to relieve our sufferings". He had arrived following the salt route. "From the mountains the Chibchas descend bringing salt and blankets, and go back up with the gold they receive", said the guide. At that very moment, gold was not so important. The first item proved of more pressing necessity. Quesada had seen his men perish on the way, pierced by poisoned arrows, plagued by implacable swarms of mosquitoes, and rotting alive from the effect of snake bites. But lack of salt was the worst of all torments, men and horses suffered from acute

Market in Plaza de Paloquemao, Bogotá

dehydration. If Quesada was unaware of the effects of a low-sodium diet, he was all too familiar with the horrible sensation of a pasty mouth. Possibly, had he observed the Indians who accompanied him, instead of dismissing as savage ritual the addition of palm shoot ash during cooking, he might have recognized wisdom born from knowledge of the environment. For the ash, rich in potassium, counteracted the lack of sodium.

On the plateau where would grow Santa Fe, administrative center of the colony to receive the name of Nueva Granada, three armies arrive, within weeks of each other, with different nutritional solutions. Their subsistence diet defines their character. Quesada, having left Santa Marta through the Magdalena river and the jungles of Carare and Opón, where "there are more snakes than trees", arrives with a decimated army, which only survived the ascent by eating the horses that died on the way. Belalcázar leads a gaudy caravan: Inca warriors wearing many-colored feather headdresses and bright robes, followed by porters chained to each

Landscape of the Sabana de Bogotá

other neck to neck. In the rearguard, pigs are carried in bamboo cages, to be slaughtered when hunger commands. Of the three, Federmann proves to be the most practical. His small troop is announced by the clucking of chickens carried in baskets by the soldiers. Were the Germans perhaps following a century-old tradition of eating eggs for breakfast on Sundays? In any case, they left a trail strewn with chicken coops.

The Indians carry their supplies in *mochilas* hanging from their shoulders. De Las Casas defines their food as "poor" and "wretched". The conquistadors find it frankly disgusting, and, to make things worse, from Mexico to Peru, their tongues and palates are scorched by the omnipresent chili. Chroniclers describe the local

fare, in highly Christian terms, as "humble" or "coarse". As for drink, the situation is just as terrible. In the absence of wine, the Spaniards are forced to down fermented palm sap. Or *chicha*, made from corn chewed with the saliva and teeth of old Indian women, who spit the mush out and let it ferment. To the list of sins already known to the wise, the clergy now adds those caused by such beverages "invented by the demons": anger, lust, conceit and murderous passion. There was no Caribbean rum available yet for the conquistador. During 16th century wars in Europe, grape spirits were used to embolden troops in battle, and as an anaesthetic for surgery afterwards.

In the *Sabana* of Bogotá, *Licenciado* Quesada finds a society of farmers and craftsmen. A peaceful

Dawn on the Sabana de Bogotá

people of merchants, farmers, goldsmiths and weavers. An economically and politically organized group. To appease the Spaniards' hunger, nothing or very little deemed appetizing is to be found: corn, potatoes, a few roots… And fishes with long whiskers and cat-like faces that Indians dig out of the mud and for which, because of their ugliness, the Spanish soldiers immediately find an abhorred name: *capitán.*

The swamps are rife with *curí,* a rodent smaller than a rabbit, a great local delicacy. A deer not larger than a greyhound grazes in the pastures, but its meat is forbidden to commoners, and reserved for dignitaries and priests. Soon, both animals will be extinct. Fruit, plentiful in warmer lands, here are a rarity. We know today which

variety was offered to the newcomers, all belonging to the same family of *solanacea:* red and yellow berries of tantalizing aspect which, when bitten into, burn like the flames of hell: *ají,* the Colombian answer to chili. *Lulos,* a round fruit covered with soft, minute thorns, which delicately but efficiently cut the hand grasping it, like the cactus variety that Indians rub with sand to rid it of invisible thorns: the prickly pear. And then again the *curuba,* of the passiflora family, at the same time acid and sweet, and the *pomarrosa,* "pink apples" growing on "musical trees", thus called because at flowering time they are swarmed by myriads of bees.

Ships arrived in Cartagena and Santa Marta, as in Habana or Santo Domingo, after a difficult and

Street vendor with Tamales, *Bogotá*

Candy for sale at Zipaquirá

costly voyage, to supply settlers with provisions. Transporting an *arroba* of flour, a jar of oil, a cow surviving the journey, to Santa Fe, in the heart of the country, at 2,600 meters above sea level, was a titanic feat.

Two decades passed after the city was founded before a soldier with the soul of a gardener, Jerónimo de Lebrón, succeeded in growing the first wheat recorded by history. And it would take another two decades to make the building of a mill worthwhile. Meanwhile, the colonists eat *puchero madrileño* without chickpeas and with little bacon, without beef and cabbage but with potatoes, a new ingredient for the Spaniards. *Cocido* would consist of a broth of native herbs, where potatoes of different size and variety cook along with *arracacha, cubios, maíz soca* (meaning milky corn, hence *mazorca*), and some wild fowl killed by stones, as gunpowder is ever scarce and expensive. The accompanying

Oatmeal beverage street stall, Bogotá

morcilla is not *morcilla*. It lacks rice and loads of onions in the Iberian fashion, and there's not enough pig's blood available to give color and flavor. The substitute is tripe stuffed with fat, nerves and tough meat, laden with salt and cumin, a costly spice which delays putrefaction, and must bear resemblance to the *longaniza* of the Nueva Granada period.

Santa Fe expands as an administrative center. Its population is mostly composed of officials and priests. Twelve years after its foundation –ten to obtain the permission and another two for bureaucratic red tape– the first white women arrive, wives of officials, or unattached ladies: widows. By that time a *criollo* generation had been born: the *mestizos*. Contrary to what occurred in Mexico, Cuba or Santo Domingo, the *mestizo* in Nueva Granada is granted citizenship immediately and without further ado. Ecclesiastic authorities look with more reprehension and

Ingredients used for making Piquete bogotano

Selling utensils in Paloquemao, Bogotá

Fritanga for sale, Bogotá

outrage upon the mulatto, of black and white blood, and with outright contempt upon the *zambo,* fruit of tropical lust, a mixture of *mestizo* and Indian, or vice-versa. Such riffraff should eat little and badly. Indian women cook what they can, they know how to prepare *mazamorra,* a cornflour mush where potatoes emerge from the bottom of the plate like rocks.

In 1760, one cow is butchered a week in the capital. Such data are found in official records, as one of the few sources of administrative revenue is the slaughter tax. Livestock killed unrestrictedly is mostly pork. Eating meat is a luxury few can afford. In 1765, the estimate is half a pound of meat per inhabitant per week. This contrasts poorly with the countryside: slaves in the mines receive four pounds of meat per week. As salt is expensive, meat is cooked in soups for preservation. The result is *sancocho.* Even when it's not Lent, fish is a frequent dish, sold

Meat cooler, Bogotá

live: the *capitán,* succulent member of the lamprey family.

In 1810, when independence from Spain is proclaimed, Santa Fe shelters a representative population. There are 16 monasteries, nine convents for cloistered nuns, a total of 650 people counting novices, servants and students. Twenty four Negro slaves, 208 military men, not counting auxiliary staff. The total population, with the facilities of a public market, fourteen churches, a hospital, two barracks, a college and "sufficient classrooms", adds up to 12,000 inhabitants at the most. There are 68 registered permanent merchants, of which 19 *chicha* outlets, 34 market stalls and 130 shops authorized to perform varied crafts, including "blacksmiths, weavers, and similar craftsmen", and 39 tailors. No boarding houses are registered, as they did not require a license.

Without doubt, meals were served on Santa Fe market

Aji for sale, Bogotá

Fruit for sale at the Siete de Agosto market place, Bogotá

places. In the stalls, broths are steaming, plantains frying, *mazorcas* goldening, potatoes boiling, black puddings simmering. Coriander is chopped on boards redolent from afar of onion and garlic. *Criollo* potatoes bask in sizzling lard, and tripe *chunchullos* roast over charcoal, which confers them a taste of the wilds.

Maids carry off the baskets that madam manages to fill after much bargaining. Wives come to buy, husbands come to nibble. Like voracious little birds, the latter peck here and there, a hundred times over. The distance between Santa Fe and the closest warm lands is one day on muleback. So there cannot be many tropical products available. No tomatoes, no oranges, no guavas, no hearts of palm. If there are any, they must be at an exorbitant price. All the better, then, to take maximum advantage of the produce at hand: to cook over the fire three types of potato, the yellow one which dissolves and gives color,

Selling cotudos, *a local biscuit in Monserrate*

the white grainy one which thickens the broth, and the other variety which retains a toothsome consistency. The dish is called *ajiaco,* and a chicken is sacrificed in its honor. Finally, in a reversed process of *criollización,* capers and fresh cream are added to the native dish.

Neither were milk and milk products frequently found on tables in the old city, except in the homes of families which owned *haciendas* near the capital. Cowherds are scarce and transportation complicated. Calves have to be suckled, and their growth is more important than the economic profits of milking. Any milk left is made into *cuajada* and fresh cheese, that *campesinos* take to the city. Waste not, want not, sour milk, a common occurrence, is cooked with *panela,* and the resulting sweet called *mielmesabe.*

Chicken is a frequent item in the diet of the *Santafereño.* Better still, the hen, which is eaten when its egg-laying days

Arepas *stall in Parque Nacional, Bogotá*   *Butcher shop in Bogotá*

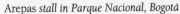

are over. In houses in the city center, the third patio is reserved for chicken pens and vegetable gardens. The fowls sleep on the branches of the *brevo,* the local name for the fig tree, the fruits of which, in syrup or *melao de panela,* are a popular dessert, along with the apples and peaches growing alongside, and the plums from the second patio. *Santafereños* who have passed the midcentury mark may recall how an expert cook, *la del dulce,* came to work several days a week in their homes, concocting syrups, chopping orange rinds for English-style marmalade, spooning the seeds out of *uchuvas* and stirring in the pan *arequipe:* milk evaporated with sugar.

Until well into the 20th century, there is no refined sugar in Colombia, except when imported from the Caribbean islands at prohibitive prices. Bread is made from corn, if there is *cuajada* or fresh cheese. Otherwise, there is no bread but golden yellow *arepas* toasted over glowing coals. Only when a mill is built in the late 18th century, on the foothills of Montserrate, using a spring which

supplies the city with drinking water, will the usual wheatbread become a staple. The flour is coarse and has to be sifted several times. With the remaining husks *cuchuco* is cooked, a measly soup reserved for students and soldiers.

Despite all these limitations, the people of Bogotá spend their time eating. Here's what could be a typical mid-nineteenth century daily fare: at 6 a.m., a shot of *aguardiente,* followed by a potato broth or *changua,* accompanied with corn or cassava bread, *arepas* and hot chocolate, thick because ground with flour; at 11 a.m., *onces,* or earlier *medias nueves,* a syrupy sweet, fresh fruit, cake and biscuit; at 2 p.m., lunch, soup, potatoes, fish or meat, tart, stewed fruit, coffee; at 6 p.m., supper, soup, eggs, fish or meat, fried corn, boiled *panela* water; at 10 p.m., dinner, hot chocolate or broth, meat, potatoes, rice, tart, corn bread, fresh or stewed fruit, cheese and a last shot of *aguardiente.*

Until the mid-twentieth century, meals are divided into several courses. Fruit is served at the beginning, following a custom some believe of

Catalan origin. Then a piping-hot soup, laced with fiery *ají,* to boost the sensation of restorative warmth and offset the city's cold and humid climate. After this comes the *seco,* consisting of potatoes, rice and meat, accompanied by an *entrada* or *principio,* vegetables cooked in milk or baked in a mold. Only tardily did vegetables enter the *Santafereño* diet through the infuence of non-Spanish Europeans, who grew them along with aromatic herbs, which performed, as in the case of bay leaves, other functions than crowning poets and generals with laurels.

By the forties, signs advertising hot meals in local restaurants were run-of-the-mill, specially for patrons. On Sundays and holidays: *cocido.* On other days: plantain soup, corn, barley or wheat *cuchuco,* flavored with cabbage, pig bones and in more generous versions with broad beans, peas and unpealed *criollo* potatoes; pearled barley or bread soup. As *seco,* rice, potatoes, meat ragout, stewed squash, potato salad, tart. And to conclude, fruit preserves with *panela,* or *cuajada con melao.* Culinary novelties and changes come from many sources. After *Independencia* the influence of French culture was enormous. If a good part of Colombian law is based on the Napoleonic Code, and if local medicine and literature is inspired by the French, small wonder that our first cookbooks follow the same model. However, after the First World War, the influence of the United States proliferates in all fields, economic as well as cultural.

Corabastos *market, Bogotá*

Street vendor in barrio Egipto, Bogotá *Fruit juice stall in Parque Nacional, Bogotá* *Fruit stall in Barrio Restrepo, Bogotá*

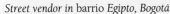

In the early twenties, eating pasta has become a national habit, after manufacturing plants are established in towns throughout the country. The arrival of European Jews fleeing from Hitler's Germany and the outbreak of the Second World War enrich the country's gastronomic palette. Factories of canned products and sausages spring up. Bakeries and pastry shops become more professionally managed. Restaurants offering international cuisine make their appearance. Airplanes make fresh fish and seafood available in places far from the coast. Tea parlors prosper, where one can indulge in biscuits, tarts and cakes of the best German and Austrian tradition. And coffee, the great source of dividends, is gaining ground over chocolate. The *Santafereño* tradition of the *tertulia,* or social gathering, over a cup of foamy hot cocoa, now occurs in a public place: the café, where one now consumes *tinto,* as *Bogotanos* call black coffee.

Nothing can hold back culture, and food is one of its manifestations. Its history is made of change. Foreign foods, coming into contact with local culinary traditions, give birth to new dishes and new tastes.

Capitals rarely eschew the condition of administrative and economic centers which attract and incorporate people from all horizons. Of the tranquil city that was Bogotá until the late thirties, when a census counted 347,615 inhabitants, little is left.

So just as one spoke yesterday of the *criollización* of Spanish customs, tomorrow one will comment on a bedlam of customs and habits, coexisting and breeding new styles.

A future analysis may well show that a so-called typical dish arriving at a table in next century's Bogotá actually turns out to be a combination of foreign contributions, and it's a moot point whether the latter come from Germany or the province of Huila.

In the ritziest restaurants and clubs, as in the humblest tienda or tejo field, fritanga makes its appetizing presence felt, genuine symbol indeed of regional gastronomy. Occasional treat in the former and daily fare in the latter, this mixture of meats, cracklings, sausages, plantains and criollo potatoes, the lot unfailingly fried in lard, represents a crowning culinary glory which fully deserves nationwide recognition.

Baked sobrebarriga *with potatoes with cheese and tomatoes*

Mixed grill

Refined sugar has only been produced in Colombia since the late 19th century. Because of this, fruits preserved in syrup are only slightly more ancient than our grandmother's grandmothers. These sweets reflect Spanish tradition, enriched by the unequalled taste of tropical fruit.

Stewed tomate de árbol

Blackberries, Peaches and Green papayuelas in syrup

Until the middle of the present century, the Santafereño custom of a chocolate reforzado afternoon snack was tantamount to a compulsory ritual among all classes of society. Bread accompanied the cup of hot chocolate in humble homes, while tamales, cheeses and fancy pastries were served in dining rooms graced with fine china.

Meringues

Traditional Santa Fe hot chocolate

Bread soup in casserole, fortifying, hearty and suited to the cold climate of the Sabana, remains piping hot until the moment of eating, because the earthenware vessel keeps it at the same temperature as the gates of hell, to quote Dante, and many an impatient glutton burns his tongue with the first spoonfuls.

Bread soup in casserole

Ajiaco santafereño

8 portions

6 chicken breasts
3 stalks of green onion
2 bay laurel leaves
1 sprig of coriander
salt and pepper to taste
12 cups (96 fl oz/3 l) water
2 bunches of guascas
2 lb (1 kg) of pastuso *potatoes*
1 1/2 lb (750 g) of sabanero *potatoes*
1 lb (500 g) of criollo *potatoes, peeled*
4 tender ears of corn, cut into segments
1 cup capers
1 cup (4 oz/120 gr) cream
4 medium avocados

*C*ook the chicken breasts with the green onions, the bay laurel leaves, the coriander, adding salt and pepper to the water, for 30 minutes. Take out the chicken and set aside.
❧ Strain the broth, and remove the grease. Put a bunch of *guascas* in the strained broth and allow to boil.
❧ Add the *pastuso* potatoes, cut into chunks. 15 minutes later add the *sabanero* potatoes, and last the *criollo* potatoes and the corn. Simmer for 20 minutes.

❧ Add the second bunch of *guascas* and continue simmering on low for ten more minutes, or until achieving the desired consistency. Remove the *guascas*.
❧ Bone and shred the chicken. Add a little warm broth to the chicken and serve separately. The capers, the cream and the avocados should also be served separately.

Piquete bogotano

8 portions

3 lb (1 1/2 kg) meaty pig's backbone
16 cups (128 fl oz/4 l) of water
salt and pepper to taste
1/4 lb (125 g) of hibias
1 lb (500 g) of small sabanero *potatoes*
1/4 lb (125 g) of peas, in their pods
1/4 (125 g) of broad beans
3 ears of corn, cut into segments
1 lb (500 g) of small criollo *potatoes*
1/4 (125 g) of cubios
3 ripe plantains peeled and cut into chunks
3 cups of hogo (see page 78)

*C*ook the pig's backbone in water with salt and pepper for 45 minutes.
❧ Add the *hibias,* the *sabanero* potatoes, the peas (still in their pods), the broad beans and the corn. Cook 20 minutes over medium heat.
❧ Add the *criollo* potatoes and the *cubios,* and cook 20 minutes more.
❧ In a separate pot cook the plantains in water for 20 minutes.
❧ Remove the pig's backbone and all the other ingredients. Strain the broth and reserve.
❧ Cut the pig's backbone into pieces and serve on a platter with the other ingredients, lavishly covered in *hogo.*

Avocado ají

Ají de aguacate

8 portions

Ají *to taste*
salt to taste
2 avocados
2 stalks green onion, finely chopped
4 tablespoons coriander, finely chopped
2 hard-boiled eggs

*C*rush the *ajíes* with the salt.
❧ Mash the avocados with a wooden spoon. Add the onion and the coriander and the grated hard-boiled eggs. Mix with the *ajíes* and salt.
❧ Mix all the ingredients together well and serve immediately.

Herb ají

Ají de hierbas

8 portions

2 ajíes
salt to taste
1/4 cup (2 oz/50 ml) vinegar
2 stalks green onion
1 onion
1 peeled tomato
2 tablespoons coriander

*C*rush the *ajíes* with the salt. Put in the vinegar and set aside for 30 minutes.
❧ Finely chop all the other ingredients and mix together with the vinegar.

Egg ají

Ají de huevo

8 portions

2 ajíes
salt to taste
2 tablespoons vinegar
1 tablespoon coriander
4 hard-boiled eggs
1/2 teaspoon lemon

*C*rush the *ajíes* with the salt and pour in the vinegar. Set aside for 30 minutes.
❧ Finely chop the coriander and the eggs
❧ Mix all the ingredients together.

Stewed tomate de árbol

Dulce de tomate de árbol

8 portions

16 ripe tomates de árbol
4 cups (32 fl oz/1 l) water
1 lb (500 g) sugar
1 lemon

*P*eel the *tomates*, leaving the stalks.
❧ Place the fruit in boiling water for a minute to remove bitterness.
❧ Drain the *tomates*, add four cups of water, the sugar and the juice from the lemon. Cook over low heat for 20 minutes
❧ With a wooden spoon, remove any foam which collects on the surface.

Baked sobrebarriga

Sobrebarriga al horno

8 portions

6 lb (3 kg) sobrebarriga (flank steak)
3 stalks of green onions, diced
3 onions, diced
4 garlic cloves, chopped
1 sprig of fresh thyme
salt and pepper to taste
6 tablespoons oil
4 carrots, peeled and cut in four
4 bay laurel leaves
1 bunch parsley
oil
1 beer (24 fl oz/750 ml)
string

Trim the meat of excess fat.
❧ Mix the onions, the garlic, the thyme, and the salt and pepper. Add the oil.
❧ Season the meat by rubbing it with this marinade. Roll the meat up and tie with the string. Marinate overnight.
❧ Cook the meat in plenty water with the carrots, the bay laurel leaves, the parsley and two tablespoons of salt until it is tender. This should take 40 minutes in a pressure cooker or about three hours in a conventional pot.

❧ Remove the meat and drain, place on a greased pan with the fatty part of the meat facing upward. Remove the string.
❧ Pour a little beer over the meat and place in an oven preheated to 400°F for 35 minutes. Baste several times with the beer and pan juices.

Potatoes with cheese and tomatoes

Papas chorreadas

8 portions

4 lb (2 kg) of tocarreño potatoes
salt
2 cups hogo

Partially peel the potatoes.
❧ Cook in water with salt for 25 minutes until they are tender.
❧ Place the potatoes on a platter and drench with very hot hogo.

Hogo

3 tablespoons oil
3 ripe tomatoes, peeled and diced
6 stalks of long green onions, chopped
5 oz (150 g) of butter or natas (skins skimmed from boiling milk)
5 oz (150 g) of fresh country cheese, grated
salt and pepper to taste

Sauté in oil the tomatoes and the onions for ten minutes.
❧ Add the butter, or natas, the cheese, the salt and the pepper and cook over low heat for an additional ten minutes.

Mixed grill

Fritanga

*N*othing is more typical of the capital's *"criollo* epicureanism" than her majesty the *fritanga,* loved and revered by all *Bogotanos.* In the ritziest restaurants and clubs, as in the humblest *tiendas* and *tejo* courts, *fritanga* imposes itself as an authentic symbol of regional gastronomy. An occasional treat in the former and daily fare in the latter, this mixed grill, unfailingly fried in lard, fully deserves nation-wide recognition. Pork is the main element, in many forms: cracklings, black puddings, loin, ribs, ears, tail and *longaniza* sausages. It is accompanied by *criollo* potatoes and plantains, the lot served on chinaware or plantain leaf, depending on the trencherman's status. Today, all over the country, carnivals, bazaars, village feasts, popular and sportive events take place amidst the tantalizing fumes wafting from stalls and tents displaying, in resplendent and colorful fashion, the sizzling palette of *fritanga.*

Meringues

Merengues

8 portions

8 egg whites
1 pinch cream of tartar
several drops of lemon juice
1/2 lb (300 g) of sugar
1/2 teaspoon vanilla or anise essence

*B*eat the egg whites into a froth with the cream of tartar.
❧ Add the drops of lemon juice. Add the sugar gradually while beating the egg whites.
❧ When the egg whites are firm add the vanilla or anise essence.
❧ Place spoonfuls of the egg whites on a greased tin. Put into an oven preheated to 350°F for ten minutes.
❧ Turn off the oven and wait a long while before taking out the meringues, so that they don't deflate, and in order to give them a crisp, golden crust.
❧ A pastry cloth-mold may be used to create different shapes if so desired.

Blackberries in syrup
Dulce de mora

8 portions

1 lb (500 g) of blackberries
1/2 cup (4 fl oz/125 ml) water
1 lb (500 g) of sugar

Clean and wash the blackberries.
❧ Place the blackberries to cook in the water and sugar for ten minutes.
❧ Use a wooden spoon to remove any foam that forms on the surface.

Peaches in syrup
Dulce de durazno

8 portions

2 lb (1 kg) peaches
1 lemon
6 cups (48 fl oz/1.5 l) water
2 lb (1 kg) sugar

Clean the peaches, rubbing them with a sponge in order to remove the peach fuzz. Wash the fruit with cold water.

❧ Put the peaches to cook in water with the juice of the lemon until boiling.
❧ Add the sugar and stir. Cook over low heat for one-and-a-half hours until the syrup thickens.
❧ Use a wooden spoon to remove any foam that forms on the surface.

Green papayuela in syrup
Dulce de papayuela verde

8 portions

2 lb (1 kg) green papayuelas
6 cups (48 fl oz/1.5 l) water
1 lemon
1 lb (500 g) sugar

Peel the *papayuelas* and put them to cook in the water and lemon juice for 30 minutes.
❧ Add the sugar. Stir and allow to thicken over low heat during 30 minutes without stirring.
❧ With a wooden spoon remove any foam that collects on the surface.

Traditional Santa Fe hot chocolate
Chocolate santafereño

The hot chocolate as served in Santa Fe is one more example of the varied culinary uses of cacao. Mixed with *panela,* it is sublimated into an eminently comforting and aromatic beverage, the frothy consistency and flavor of which conquered the kitchens of Bogotá, the Sabana and the entire country. Until the middle of this century, the *Santafereño* custom of *chocolate reforzado* (mid-afternoon refreshment, also known as *onces*) was somewhat of a compulsory ritual for all social classes. While in the poorest homes the cup of hot chocolate was accompanied with bread or sponge cake, in more affluent dwellings *tamales,* cheese and fancy breads graced the tables. Today only nostalgia remains for this custom. But, if perchance one receives an invitation to savor a cup of hot chocolate, even only accompanied by a meager *mogolla* bun… there's no valid excuse whatsoever to turn it down!

Lime rinds in syrup

Cascos de limón en almíbar

8 portions

2 lb (1 kg) large limes
1 pinch bicarbonate of soda
8 cups (64 fl oz/2.0 l) water
1 1/2 lb (750 g) sugar
gratings from 4 limes

*S*crape the lemons on a rough surface, cut them in half and remove their pulp, taking care not to damage the peels.

❧ Put them in plenty water with the bicarbonate of soda until boiling. Discard the water.

❧ In a large, preferably copper, pan, pour the eight cups of water to heat. Add the sugar, the lemon gratings and stir.

❧ Add the lemon rinds and allow to thicken over low heat during one hour or until obtaining the desired consistency.

Bread soup in casserole

Sopa de pan en cazuela

8 portions

4 cups (32 fl oz/1 l) milk
4 cups (32 oz/1 l) basic broth (see same page)
salt and pepper to taste
2 tablespoons (1 oz/ 30 g) butter
2 garlic cloves, chopped
4 calados (toasted bread slices), crumbled
4 stale almojábanas, cut in slices
8 thin slices of white cheese
8 thin slices of white bread
8 raw eggs
8 tablespoons (1/2 cup) of cream

*P*ut the milk and broth to boil over medium heat, adding salt and pepper.

❧ Sauté the garlic and the onions in the butter, until they are soft and golden.

❧ Distribute among eight individual casseroles the crumbled *calados,* the *almojábanas,* the slices of cheese and a tablespoon full of the sautéed onions and garlic. Fill the casseroles with the broth.

❧ Place a slice of bread, a raw egg and a tablespoon of cream into each individual casserole.

❧ Put the casseroles into an oven preheated to 375ºF for five minutes, until the eggs cook. Serve immediately.

Basic broth

Caldo básico

2 lb (1 kg) of meaty bones
1 lb (500 g) marrow bones
5 cloves of garlic
2 large onions
2 stalks celery
2 bay laurel leaves
2 tablespoons parsley
2 sprigs of thyme
2 large carrots
1 large turnip
12 cups (96 fl oz/3 l) of water
salt and pepper to taste

*P*lace all of the ingredients to cook over low heat for two hours. Remove frequently the foam which collects on the surface.

❧ Remove the bones and strain the broth, which can be frozen for further use.

❧ Beef bones can be replaced by chicken or fish bones, depending on what dish the broth is to be used for.

Puchero bogotano

8 portions

16 cups (128 fl oz/4 l) of water
1 lb (500 g) of boneless beef, cut into
   chunks
1/2 lb (300 g) of beef ribs
4 bay laurel leaves
4 garlic cloves, chopped
4 onions
2 sprigs thyme
salt and pepper to taste
1 chicken cut in pieces
1 lb (500 g) of boneless pork, cut into
   chunks
1/2 lb (300 g) of pork ribs
1/2 lb (250 g) of bacon, diced
1 lb (500 g) of longaniza pork sausage
3 green plantains
3 ears of corn, husked and cut into
   segments
1 1/2 lb (750 g) of sabanero potatoes
10 cabbage leaves
1 1/2 lb (750 g) of cassava
2 ripe plantains
1 small chunk of panela
2 cups hogo (see page 78)

Cut the beef fillet and ribs, the pork loin and ribs, the bacon and *longaniza* into small pieces.

Crush the garlic, cut the onions in two, peel and slice the plantains, potatoes and cassava.

Cook over medium heat for 30 minutes the beef fillet and ribs with the bay laurel, the garlic, the onion and the thyme. Add salt and pepper.

Add the chicken, the pork loin and ribs, the bacon, the *longaniza* and cook for one more hour.

Remove the different meats making sure that they are now tender. Set aside.

Add the green plantains and corn to the broth, and allow to cook over low heat for 15 minutes.

Add the potatoes, the cabbage, the cassava and allow to boil for 20 minutes.

Wash the ripe plantains, removing their tips. Cook in water with the little chunk of *panela* for 20 minutes.

Put the various meats into the broth for five minutes in order to heat them up.

Peel the cooked ripe plantain and cut it in pieces.

Remove all the ingredients from the broth and distribute the ingredients on individual plates, adding pieces of the ripe plantain, peeled and cut into chunks.

Place one cabbage leaf on top of each plate and drench with hot *hogo*.

Strain the broth and serve separately.

Curuba iced drink

Sorbete de curuba

8 portions

8 ripe curubas
1 cup (250 g/ 1/2 lb) sugar
1 liter (32 oz) milk

*C*ut open the *curubas* and remove the pulp, add two tablespoons of sugar and set aside for ten minutes to release the juice.
❧ Mix the *curuba* pulp in a blender with the rest of the sugar. Strain the juice.
❧ Mix with ice-cold milk and beat to a froth.

Tomate de árbol iced drink

Sorbete de tomate de árbol

8 portions

10 ripe tomates de árbol
2 cups (16 fl oz/1/2 l) water
1 liter (32 fl oz) of milk
1 cup (250g/1/2 l) sugar

*P*eel the tomates and boil them in water for three minutes.
❧ Mix the fruit in a blender with a cup of the water they were boiled in. Strain and add the sugar.
❧ Mix in the blender again, at low speed, adding the cold milk slowly to avoid curdling.

Following page: Tamales *and* Empanadas de pipián, *with Peanut* ají

Gran Cauca

During the colonial period and the early days of the Republic, "the Province of Cauca" covered practically one third of the map of Colombia. It has always been an administrative rather than geographic region, which reflects in its cuisine. Local culture is a result of the combination of ethnic groups with the environment, Indians, whites of Spanish extraction, African Negroes, the lot mixed together over five centuries.

The most influential city during the colonial period was Popayán, embedded in the thickest Andes, and a natural stopover on the road to Ecuador and Peru. Popayán was a wealthy city because of the large gold-bearing zones under its administration, and mining represented the main source of revenue for the Spanish Empire.

The region is geographically varied and rich in contrasts. Most of the country's active volcanoes lie in this part of the Andes. It is a rugged territory, with large humid as well as dry expanses. It includes high-altitude Andean rainy woodlands, known as *páramos*, a habitat unique on the planet,

Market in Santander de Quilichao

tropical rain forests on the slopes and plains of the Western Cordillera facing the Pacific, and the immense and fertile valleys bathed by the Cauca river.

Native civilizations were as varied as its territory. The Tumacos were wonderful ceramists; the Calimas, consummate goldsmiths; the Paeces and Guambianos, experienced farmers. Only to mention a few, the list is too long.

Contrary to what happened in other parts of the country, large Indian groups survived and maintained their culture's characteristics, or absorbed alien ways into their world. In some cases, the natives taught the newcomers how to handle the environment in order to make life conditions easier and better. In other words, they made a *criollo* out of the foreigner.

To a certain extent, in the Gran Cauca region, *mestizos* and mulattoes, Indians and Negroes, Whites now of *Caucano* instead of Spanish heritage, share the same world and choose their preferences within a common repertoire. And there can be no better example than cooking.

Tamales de pipián laced with peppery peanut sauce are an Andean inheritance. Oil, as a basic vehicle for frying instead of lard, seems to be a contribution of Negro ethnic groups, which extracted it from oleaginous palm fruits, as in their native lands. One owes to slaves the use of the *chontaduro,* a fruit of the palm family, in the preparation of which white man probably intervened, with *panela* produced in his sugar mills. The addition of salt and *panela* to the cooking of the fruit must be relatively new, because the first sugar mills were installed in the late eighteenth century.

For an attentive reader, *María,* the novel by Jorge Isaacs, would prove instrumental to understand the influence of French romanticism on Latin American literature and on Negro cuisine in Gran Cauca. Flocking around the heroines always impeccably dressed in white, the Negresses, whose realm is the kitchen, go to and fro with tablewares, prepare balms for the throes of love and the miseries of indifference, with no mysteries other than culinary care, the aroma of freshness and the delight of a lovingly-done task. Breads made of corn and cassava flour rise in the oven thanks to their heart of soft cheese; crunchy toasted plantain slices; round coconut sweets; salty pork cracklings to accompany the mysteriously sweet taste of beans cooked with plantain. One owes Negro culture such envigorating and strange jungle fruit as the *borojó,* allegedly of potent aphrodisiac properties. More difficult to trace is a typical Valle province

Oxen near Pasto, Nariño

Gorgona Island in the Pacific Ocean

Market on the Atrato river in Quibdo, Chocó

dessert: *manjar blanco,* a milk sweet laced with rice flour. Historically, it may well originate from Spain, except that it is preserved in a calabash, the most Latin American recipient imaginable.

In the Cauca valley, cooking is the business of Black women. Under the volcano Puracé, in Popayán, the *Ñapangas,* pure *criolla* women because they are neither Spanish nor Indian, are in charge of the kitchen. Hence the ubiquitous indigenous sauce made with milk, onions and peanuts, to accompany yellow potatoes and steamed chicken over ferns, as game was cooked on the *páramos.* The same women concoct the *tamales de pipián,* made with the dough of *criollo* potatoes and *hogo* wrapped in plantain leaves, and fry crisp, half-moon shaped *empanadas* stuffed, yet again, with *pipián,* to be soused in peppery peanut sauce, as an appetizer before heartier dishes.

On the Pacific coast, in Buenaventura, Tumaco and the Chocó rain forests, a Latin American savor enhanced by reminiscences of Africa is dominant: shrimps, prawns and tuna trapped in the Humboldt Current, and white or dark-fleshed snook, all either consumed locally or exported.

Pasto, a city north of the border between Colombia and Ecuador, is radically different from the gastronomical point of view. Its cuisine results from a geographical and cultural background which is a wholly Indian domain. Seen from the air, the cordillera stretches of Nariño province look like a patchwork quilt, of an all-pervading green. At ground level, the perspective changes: beauty vanishes into the minuteness of farms… So little land for so many people… *Campesinos* and their families eke a livelihood from such a meager lot. The harvest sold, little is left to eat, let alone time to think about improving on a dish.

In the history of Colombia, during the struggle to achieve independence, Pasto became the stronghold of the Spanish Crown and Empire. Tradition, with all its cultural inertia, hinders change. Pasto and its surrounding territories defended the established order. And something similar must have happened in their kitchens,

Picking potatoes in Tuquerres, Nariño

Planting sugarcane. Cauca Valley

stubbornly clinging to sempiternal tradition: an obsessive native partiality to *cui* meat and *pucheros,* to the exclusion of other delicacies.

Without any industrial demand, milk remained a domestic product, the cream used for making butter and cottage cheese.

During Colonial and a good part of Republican times, Popayán was the prominent cultural center, where all roads and communications converged. The city withheld its leadership of soldiers and scholars until Cali, located on the fertile plains of the Cauca river valley and in a strategic position between the capital and the Pacific harbors, imposed its greater prosperity.

Cali emerged in Colombia's economic history in the late nineteenth century, when agriculture and industry were integrated by the first sugar mills.

Unlike Popayán, where the upper-class rested securely upon land holdings, the *Caleño* oligarchy develops its power on a

Guambiano Indians from Silvia, Cauca

basis of technical competence. Settlement in the area is due to local immigration attracted by work opportunities. Small wonder, then, that a good part of *Valluna* culinary specialities, *pandebono* for example, like *cucas* and *panderos* are more an industrial than domestic product.

The melting pot of new cities with mushrooming populations creates a varied palette of tastes, tainted by nostalgia. Time and available ingredients will eventually give the desired flavor to the local dish one yearns for. And here lies the crucial role played by new generations in its elaboration. The traditional comes to be more a question of form than content.

It is not easy to determine at which point *arroz atollado* became a regional dish of the Cauca valley. Under the same name, *atollado,* meaning "done in a jiffy" or "let's get it over with", was a popular *Santafereño* kind of *paella:* rice with sausages and vegetables, of a dry or moist

Grilled trout with puffed potatoes

Selling fruit and juices on the street. Cali, Cauca Valley

texture. The *atollado valluno* is more of a soup, but in a befuddling combination of solid and liquid texture. Green giant plantain slices, fried in oil to golden crispness, are an inevitable side dish.

Hogao, an eminently *criollo* spiced-up sauce and seasoning of fried onions and tomatoes is of daily use in the region.

In a nutshell, the basic cuisine of Gran Cauca offers a riot of magnificent and varied flavors, in unison with its landscapes, where snow-capped volcanoes tower over the rainiest jungles in the world, where the aphrodisiac *borojó* grows and where more bird species dwell than anywhere else in the world.

In warm lands throughout entire Colombia, plantain enjoys the status of staple food. Cooking, which is a form of culture, sublimates this product. It can be sweet as in *abojarrados* and pastry, or salted when fried, but always splendid and intriguing.

Plantain cake, Baked plantain with cheese and Aborrajados

Rice pudding

It is not easy to determine at what moment arroz atollado *became a typical dish of the
Cauca valley. A paella of sorts, but of mushier consistence, its mysterious charm resides
in being neither soup nor paella, with the best of both textures.*

Arroz atollado *with Green plantain chips*

Shepherd's cake

By tradition, sweets from the Cauca valley display a wide spectrum of textures and complex techniques. An outstanding example is manjar blanco, made with milk and rice flour. Historically the origin is Spanish, but the gourd vessel proves eminently Latin American.

Macetas de San Antonio

Manjar blanco, Espejuelo and Confites

In hot climates, refreshments are a godsend. Water is a blessing and the addition of fruit a miracle. Sometimes fruit are given the piquant touch of early fermentation. Champús and salpicón *always haunt the dreams of the ever-thirsty* Vallecaucano.

Champús

Panderos, cucas *and* pandebonos *are made with flours as distinct as Europe, Asia and* America. Panderos *were originally made with flour from the mysterious sago palm, a tree of which only the memory is left.* Pandebonos *are made with cornflour and cheese, as are* cucas, *but with the sweet touch of panela.*

Cocadas

Chicken and oxtail stew
Sancocho de gallina y cola

8 portions

2 stalks of green onion, chopped
2 green tomatoes, diced
2 onions, finely chopped
4 garlic cloves, chopped
14 cups (112 fl oz/3.5 l) of water
2 stalks of green onion, whole
2 lb (1 kg) of oxtail, cut into segments
1 large chicken, cut into pieces
4 green plantains
1 lb (500 g) of cassava, peeled and cut into
   pieces
3 ears of corn cut into pieces
1/2 (250 g) of pumpkin, unpeeled
salt, pepper and cumin to taste
saffron
5 leaves of wild coriander
2 teaspoons of coriander, finely chopped

Chop together the green onions, the green tomatoes, and the garlic.
❧ Place the oxtail in 14 cups of water to which the green onion and green tomato mixture has been added. Cover the pot and cook high for one hour.
❧ Add the chicken and the plantain peeled and broken into pieces by hand while adding to the pot. Lower the heat to medium and simmer with the pot covered for 30 minutes.
❧ Remove the onion stalks, and add the cassava, the corn, the pumpkin, salt, pepper, cumin, saffron, wild coriander and cook for 20 more minutes.
❧ Simmer for ten minutes more over low heat. Before serving, garnish with the coriander.
❧ It is advisable to use wooden implements for stirring this dish.
❧ Accompany with ají.

Beefsteak criollo style
Bistec a la criolla

8 portions

4 lb (2 kg) beef fillet
1 tablespoon mustard
pepper and cumin to taste
2 tablespoons vinegar
oil
2 ripe tomatoes, peeled and diced
2 stalks green onions, finely chopped
2 onions, diced
2 garlic cloves, chopped
1 tablespoon of fresh oregano
salt to taste

Cut the meat into eight slices and season with the mustard, pepper, cumin and vinegar. Allow to marinate during one hour.
❧ Sauté in oil the tomatoes, the onions, the garlic, the oregano and the salt for ten minutes until obtaining an even sauce.
❧ In a little very hot oil brown the meat on both sides. Add salt and the sauce. Cover the pan and cook over medium heat for ten minutes.

Pipián tamales

Tamales de pipián

1 1/2 lb (750 g) of stale corn dough
3 tablespoons lard
1 pinch salt
lightly roasted plantain leaves
1 1/2 lb (750 g) of pipián
1 lb (500 g) of pork loin, cut into very
  small pieces
2 hard-boiled eggs, sliced
pita hemp string

*M*ix thoroughly the corn dough with the lard and the salt.
❧ Fry the meat with some salt for 20 minutes.
❧ To prepare the *tamales*: place a helping of the dough on a plantain leaf, flattening it with your fingers. In the middle of the dough put bits of the meat, the *pipián* and the eggs. Knead the dough around the mixture. Fold the plantain leaf and insert the two extremities into each other, before tying with the pita hemp string.
❧ Cook with little water in a covered pot during 30 minutes over medium heat.

Pipián empanadas

2 lb (1 kg) of stale corn dough
2 tablespoons of cassava starch
lightly roasted plantain leaves
salt to taste
2 cups pipián
oil

*M*ix the corn dough with the cassava starch and the salt until obtaining a smooth and even paste.
❧ Form the dough into balls and flatten with fingers on top of each plantain leaf, lightly roasted and greased. In the center of the dough place a teaspoon of *pipián*. Fold the leaf and seal the *empanada* into a half-moon shape with fingers.
❧ Fry in very hot oil until golden, serve with peanut *ají*.

Pipián

3 lb (1.5 kg) of criollo *potatoes*,
  peeled and diced
oil
1 stalk of green onion, diced
1 onion, diced
3 ripe tomatoes, diced
1 garlic clove, chopped
1/2 red pepper, finely chopped

salt and pepper to taste
1 tablespoon annatto
1 cup (8 oz/250 ml) basic broth (see page
  81)
1/2 cup peanuts toasted and ground
1 hard-boiled egg, diced

*C*ook the potatoes in water with salt for 15 minutes.
❧ Sauté in oil the onions, the tomatoes, the garlic, and the red peppers. Add salt and pepper.
❧ Add the annatto, basic broth and stir well. Add the cooked potatoes, peanuts and hard-boiled eggs. Mix thoroughly..

Peanut ají

1/2 cup (4 oz/125ml) basic
  broth (see page 81)
250 g of roasted and ground peanuts
1 ripe tomato, peeled and diced
2 stalks of green onion, finely chopped
6 ajíes, chopped
1 tablespoon chopped coriander
1 hard-boiled egg, chopped
1 lemon
salt to taste

*S*tir broth and peanuts, then add other ingredients.

Grilled trout

Truchas asadas

8 portions

8 trout, cleaned
4 lemons
salt
oil

*R*ub the trout all over with the
lemons. Salt the insides and baste with
oil.
❧ Barbecue them over coals on a
greased grill for 20 minutes.
❧ Turn the trout over after ten minutes
to ensure that they grill on both sides.

Puffed potatoes

Papas sopladas

8 portions

16 pastuso *or* sabanero *potatoes*
salt

*W*ash and dry the potatoes. Cut in
half lengthwise. Place face-up on tin,
cover with thin layer of salt.
❧ Place in an oven preheated to 350°F
for 20 minutes, until the potatoes puff.

Fish cebiche

Cebiche de pescado

8 portions

2 lb (1 kg) sea bass
1/2 lb (250 g) red onions, finely chopped
1 garlic clove, chopped
1/2 green pepper, finely diced
1 green tomato, finely diced
1 tablespoon ají
salt and pepper to taste
2 tablespoons vinegar
enough lemon juice to cover

*C*ut the fish into small pieces making
sure that there are no fishbones.
❧ In a glass bowl mix the fish with the
onions, the garlic, the green pepper, the
tomato, the *ají*, the salt and pepper. Stir
thoroughly with the vinegar and lemon
juice.
❧ Allow to marinate for four hours
before serving.

Prawn cebiche

Cebiche de langostinos

8 portions

40 fresh prawn, in their shells
grating from 1 orange
grating from 4 lemons
juice of 4 oranges
juice of 1 lemon
1 teaspoon sugar
salt to taste
1 tablespoon of ají
3 red onions cut into very thin slices
2 red tomatoes, finely diced
2 tablespoons coriander, finely chopped

*C*ook the prawns in boiling water for
two minutes. Toss into a colander and
rinse in fresh water.
❧ Peel the prawns without removing the
tips. Clean them.
❧ In a glass or earthenware bowl, mix
the prawns with the gratings and juice
from the lemons and oranges. Add the
sugar, the salt, the *ají*, the onion, the
tomato and the coriander.
❧ Allow to marinate for four hours
before serving.

Baked plantain with cheese

Plátano asado con queso

8 portions

4 very ripe plantains (they should have
    black skins)
2 tablespoons butter
4 oz (125 g) white cheese, cut into slices

*P*eel the plantains, slicing them
lengthwise but not all the way through.
Butter and place on greased tinfoil.
Place in an oven preheated to 350°F for
ten minutes.

❧ Remove from the oven and insert the
cheese slices in the slit plantains.
Replace in the oven and bake for an
additional ten minutes so that the
cheese melts and the plantains golden.

❧ Cut in half and serve hot.

Plantain cake

Torta de maduro

8 portions

8 ripe plantains, cooked and ground
10 oz (300 g) of white cheese, grated

6 eggs, beaten
3 tablespoons of panela, grated
4 tablespoons butter
1/2 teaspoon vanilla essence
1 teaspoon baking powder
1/2 teaspoon powdered cinnamon
1/4 teaspoon nutmeg
1 pinch salt

*M*ix all the ingredients together,
kneading by hand until obtaining a
smooth dough.

❧ Place in a buttered ovenproof mold
and put in an oven preheated to 350°F
for approximately 40 minutes.

Aborrajados

8 portions

6 very ripe plantains
oil
1/2 lb (250 g) of white cheese
3 beaten eggs
6 tablespoons of wheat flour
1 teaspoon bicarbonate of soda.
salt to taste

*P*eel the plantains and slice
diagonally.

❧ Fry the slices in very hot oil until
golden. Remove and flatten them a bit.

❧ Cut the cheese in thin slices slightly
smaller than the plantains.

❧ Beat the eggs with the three
tablespoons of wheat flour, the
bicarbonate of soda and the salt.

❧ Place a slice of cheese between two
slices of plantain. Sprinkle with flour
and dip into the egg mixture.

❧ Fry in very hot oil until golden.

Rice pudding

Arroz de leche

8 portions

3 cups (24 fl oz/750 ml) milk
1 cup (8 oz/250 ml) water
2 cups (500g/1 lb) washed rice
1/2 lb (300 g) of sugar
2 cinnamon sticks
1/2 cup raisins
1 pinch salt

$\mathcal{P}$ut the rice to cook in two cups of milk and one cup of water for 20 minutes over medium heat.

❧ When the rice begins to dry, add the rest of the milk, mixed with the sugar, the cinnamon and the raisins.

❧ Lower the heat, add a pinch of salt and stir constantly during 15 minutes.

❧ Serve hot or cold.

Arroz atollado

8 portions

12 cups (96 fl oz/3 l) water
2 lb (1 kg) pork ribs, cut into segments
1/2 lb (250 g) pork loin, diced
1 lb (500 g) longaniza sausage, sliced
1 1/2 cups hogao (see page 142)
salt to taste
1 tablespoon black peppercorns
1/2 teaspoon white pepper, ground
3 cups rice
4 tablespoons lard
1 lb (500 g) of purple potatoes, peeled and diced
2 tablespoons coriander and parsley, finely chopped
4 hard-boiled eggs, diced

$\mathcal{C}$ook in water the pork ribs and loin, with a little salt, for 30 minutes.

❧ Sauté the longaniza and add it to the broth along with half of the hogao, the rice and the lard. Season with salt and pepper. Cook over medium heat for 20 minutes.

❧ Add the potatoes, stirring well. Continue cooking low for 20 minutes, with the cover on, until the potatoes are ready.

❧ Add half the coriander and parsley, the diced eggs and stir. The rice must remain moist.

❧ Upon serving garnish each portion with a tablespoon of hogao and the rest of the chopped herbs.

Green plantain fries

Tostadas de plátano verde

8 portions

8 small and slender green plantains
oil
salt to taste

$\mathcal{P}$eel the plantains and fry them in oil not too hot until they begin to acquire a little color.

❧ Remove from the oil and place, one by one, on a damp kitchen cloth dampened with salted water. Fold the cloth over each plantain and proceed to flatten it with a large stone or rolling pin until as thin as possible.

❧ Fry the plantain in very hot oil until golden. Drain and sprinkle with salt.

Shepherd's cake

Torta de pastores

8 portions

6 cups of rice pudding (see page109)
3 cups (12 oz) of biscuit crumbs
4 1/2 tablespoons of butter
1 1/2 cups (6 oz/180 g) white cheese,
  grated
6 eggs, beaten
1 1/2 tablespoons cinnamon
1/4 lb (150 g) raisins
1 pinch nutmeg

Knead all the ingredients into a
smooth dough.
❧ Place in a greased pan and put into an
oven preheated to 350°F for one hour
until golden on top.

Macetas de San Antonio

On Sundays and festive days, in
almost all small villages of the Cauca
valley, "distinguished characters"
religiously stage their appearance in
parks and church porches, surrounded
by swarms of children mesmerized by
the marvels they display. The fabulous
merchandise are simply macetas, which
represent in the children's imagination
a "totem with lollipops and streamers"
of sorts. These are contraptions created
in simple and practical fashion by
popular inventiveness, to advertise
what children love most… sweets!
Made of dried maguey sticks, macetas
are perforated with tiny holes, from
which hang sugarcane-fiber strings with
dangling candy silhouettes of horses,
dogs, ducks or flowers. An added treat
for the children resides in the countless
and gaudy paper strips decorating the
macetas, crowned with whirlygigs in
perpetual motion, adding magic to the
lure of sweets.

Manjar blanco

1/4 cup rice
6 liters milk
4 lb (2 kg) sugar
salt
150 g of raisins
3 black figs in syrup, cut into slivers

Soak the rice for two days.
❧ Drain, grind and dissolve the rice in
milk, add the sugar and salt.
❧ Cook high, and stir constantly until
the bottom of the pot is visible, add the
raisins and remove from the fire.
❧ Spoon into individual bowls and
decorate the surface with the black fig
slivers.

Salpicón de Baudilia

8 portions

1/2 pineapple, finely diced
3 lulos, *chopped and strained*
1/2 papaya, diced
1/4 soursop, *without seeds*
6 piñuelas, *peeled and diced*
1/2 lb (250 g) of blackberries,
    mashed and strained
8 cups (64 fl oz/ 2 l) water
1/2 lb (250 g) sugar
crushed ice

$\mathcal{M}$ix the fruit with the sugar, add the water and stir thoroughly.
❧ Serve immediately with lots of crushed ice.

Champús

1 lb (500 g) of shelled corn
14 cups (112 fl oz/3.5 l) liters water
1 pineapple, peeled and finely-diced
1 loaf of panela
6 bitter orange leaves
6 cloves
5 cinnamon sticks
pulp of 12 lulos
crushed ice

$\mathcal{C}$ook the corn in water for approximately one hour.
❧ When the corn is tender, take one-and-a-half cup of corn from the pot and grind. Put the ground corn again in the water and stir until dissolving.
❧ Take one cup of this solution and mix in the blender with half the pineapple. Return the mixture to the pot.
❧ Put the *panela* in one cup of water along with the bitter orange leaves, the cloves and the cinnamon, and cook into a syrup.
❧ Dissolve this syrup into the corn-mush and add the *lulo* pulp and the rest of the pineapple, squeezed together with your hands.
❧ Stir everything together thoroughly and add crushed ice.

Cocadas

2 grated coconuts
water from 2 coconuts
1 1/2 lb (750 g) sugar
4 ground cloves
1 lemon

$\mathcal{C}$ook the grated coconut in its own water over medium heat with 250 g of sugar and the ground cloves.
❧ When the syrup starts to thicken, add the rest of the sugar and the juice from the lemon. Stir with a wooden spoon until the mixture thickens and darkens.
❧ With the wooden spoon take out small coconut shreds and place on a damp tray. Allow to cool.
❧ The color of the *cocadas* varies according to what degree the syrup is allowed to burn.

Cucas

1 cup (8 fl oz/250 ml) water
8 cloves
1 tablespoon cinnamon
1 black panela
2 lb (1 kg) wheat flour
8 oz (250 g) butter
4 eggs, beaten
1 teaspoon baking powder
1 pinch bicarbonate of soda, dissolved
  in a little warm milk
1 tablespoon gratings from the peels of an
  orange and a lemon
1 tablespoon burnt panela
butter

𝒫ut the water to boil with the
cinnamon and the cloves. Strain, add
the *panela* and cook for 30 minutes
until obtaining a thick syrup. Allow to
cool.
❧ Mix the flour, the butter, the eggs, the
lemon and orange gratings, the
bicarbonate of soda and the baking
powder. Knead into a smooth dough.
❧ Add the syrup and a spoonful of
burnt *panela,* blending them well in.
❧ Place the dough on a wooden table
sprinkled with flour, flatten with a
rolling pin, cut out circles of about ten
centimeters in diameter, put on greased
tinfoil and bake at 350°F for 20
minutes.

Panderos

2 lb (1 kg) cassava starch
3 cups panela syrup (see page 161)
4 eggs, beaten
1/2 teaspoon salt
1/2 teaspoon baking powder
4 oz (125 g) of butter
1 cup aguardiente

𝓜ix all the ingredients together
until obtaining a smooth dough.
❧ Spread the dough on a wooden table
sprinkled with flour. Twist strips of
dough into snail-like spirals about the
size of a cookie.
❧ Place on greased tinfoil and put in an
oven preheated to 350°F for 25 minutes
until golden.

Pandebono

2 cups of threshed-corn dough
1 cup of (sour) cassava starch
3 cups of white salty cheese, grated
3 cups fresh cottage cheese
2 eggs, beaten

𝓜ix all the ingredients in a wooden
bowl and knead into a smooth dough.
❧ Shape the dough into balls and place
separately on greased tinfoil. Put into
an oven preheated to 350°F for 20
minutes, until the *pandebonos* rise and
turn golden.

Guinea-pig

Cui

8 portions

8 cuis
6 lemons
salt and pepper to taste
1 thick green onion stalk
oil

Slaughter the *cuis* by slitting their throats. Bleed them by hanging for one hour.

❧ Parboil them and remove the hair with your hands, then scrape with a knife until clean, slit open and gut. Wash well in water and lemon, scrub hard to remove the musk.

❧ Make a small incision in the belly. Introduce a finger carefully into the slit and separate the skin from the flesh. Sprinkle with salt and set aside for one hour. Wash well with water and dry. There are various methods of preparation:

❧ Traditionally *cuis* are skewered lengthwise on a thin stick supported by two forked prongs planted in the ground. The animals are roasted over a fire kindled beneath, for approximately an hour, turned slowly and basted with a green onion stalk dipped in oil.

❧ They can also be prepared in an oven. Baste the *cuis* with oil and bake in a greased pan for 40 minutes in an oven preheated to 400°F. Baste again and flip over occasionally.

❧ Ten minutes before they are done, sprinkle with lemon juice.

❧ Another fashion is to cut and stew them for 15 minutes over low heat in *hogao* and enough water to cover. Remove and grill over charcoal or fry in sizzling oil until golden.

Following page: Natilla *and* Buñuelos

Antioquia
and Viejo Caldas

A look at the map shows the original geographical situation of Antioquia: the Central Cordillera, its foothills and valleys, the soils of which are mostly formed by a layer of lava and ashes from the Ruiz and Tolima volcanoes, on a base of granites and bedrock rich in gold and silver, squeezed between tertiary sandstone and clay. Under the administrative division of the Colony, a great part of the territory now known as Antioquia belonged to the province of Cauca. The Cauca river was the most natural access towards the richest gold fields discovered by the conquistadors. Through the valley of the Cauca river came Negro slaves to replace Indians wiped out by overwork and disease. During the Colonial and a good part of the Republican eras, most of the gold was extracted on slopes of the Western Cordillera facing the Pacific, in what is today called the Chocó. The gold, of alluvium and not lode origin, was obtained by *mazamorreando,* panwashing sands. Santa Fe de Antioquia became the trading center, and the precious metal was

Food store, Manizales, Caldas

shipped through the Cauca and Magdalena rivers on to Cartagena.

In Antioquia, miners did not necessarily own their plots; more often they exploited them with or without a licence, formed into mobile outfits led by an administrator or his overseers. Such bands purchased food and supplies in neighboring towns, and carried them to the work zone on the backs of mules or Negroes. Attracted by sales prospects and miners' purchasing power, traders flocked to such centers, followed by farmers and cattlemen who replenished their stores.

In 1860, in the Aburrá valley, 1,400 meters above sea level, a town of traders and farmers begins to grow. The town is called Medellín. Until the 18th century, it occupies a secondary rank compared with Santa Fe de Antioquia, Rionegro or Zaragoza. It takes two weeks in the best of conditions to reach the capital of the Viceroyalty. The traveller, if wealthy, is seated in a chair carried on the back of an Indian, more sure-footed than a mule, who crosses obstacles on the road and walks on tiptoes over tree trunks bridging abysses over turbulent mountain streams. He will then climb up to the 2,800 meter-high pass in the Eastern Cordillera before descending to the Magdalena river port of Honda (800 meters), a stretch he will have to do on horse or muleback, as it was always strictly forbidden to travel from Guaduas to Santa Fe "riding on an Indian". The journey from Medellín to the capital of the Viceroyalty takes longer than from Cartagena to Hamburg.

Visitors from Europe or the United States, upon discovering Medellín, describe in books or travel notes their impression of a city unlike any other in the New World. They find it tidy, pleasant, peaceful, and the inhabitants "courteous, hard-working and hospitable". Carl August Gosselman, a Swedish traveller who dropped by in 1825, writes:

"It is full of trees, clean and the temperature that of springtime (...). In no way can its trade be considered insignificant. Indeed the town must be seen as a warehouse for most of the province. There are no foreign trading houses, but many wealthy merchants...". Slowly, the city also becomes a manufacturing center, and soon provides credit to support production and trade. Families are large. Safray tells: "It is not unusual to find families with over a dozen children, all of them well fed". He further adds: "In the market, there is an abundance of corn, sold in the form of *arepas* and thick, succulent biscuits. Wheat bread is a luxury item only eaten with hot chocolate. The Spaniards found the *arepa* disgusting. Nowadays rich and poor eat it with relish".

Bamboo and cambulo *woodlands near Armenia, Quindío*

Wax palms in Quindío

Coffee pickers in Bolombolo, Antioquia

Colonization spreads from the settlements. Men go looking for gold and leave their families behind as a support base. To provide for themselves, they cut down entire jungles and plant corn along with beans. They fatten pigs with corn and plantain. Sometimes they work two weeks in the mines and return to their land with sufficient food to support families for another two weeks. Others, treasure-hunters instead of miners, look for *guacas,* Indian burial sites full of riches. Enormous zones were opened up by these fortune-seekers. The Gold Museum of the Banco de la República contains some of these treasures, specifically from the local Quimbaya and Tolima cultures.

As they make their progress inland, the colonists found villages which are used in turn as supply centers. In cold lands corn and beans are harvested once a year, and in warm lands twice a year. This was the major factor which drove colonists towards hotter climates.

In 1880, the price of coffee soars, creating export opportunities. Gold and commerce have created groups in Antioquia with wealth in cash instead of land. Attracted by good business prospects, these entrepeneurs buy land in the concessions and organize settlements. They finance the colonist who lacks funds but can pay his debt in labor.

Families of coffee-growers settle on plots not exceeding 24 hectares, that they farm themselves. The coffee *finca* is an economic unit, which grows what it needs and sells the surplus, almost always transported by mule, an animal to later become part of the advertising image of Colombian coffee.

It becomes imperative to open up roads through jungles and mountain cliffs. Colonization involves a huge collective effort, where everyone participates. To make it possible, food has to be provided for hundreds. Pioneers and traders create pasturelands for up to 60,000 heads of cattle and enclosures for the herds of pigs which accompany the bands of laborers. Antioquia and its people make their appearance in the world thanks to a capacity for enterprise and finance which must

Plantain loads in Armenia, Quindío

Coffee picker in Bolombolo, Antioquia

have seemed reckless in the 19th century. Railways, steamship companies on difficult rivers, bridges were established, and an aerial cable was even suspended to carry coffee directly and cheaply from Manizales to Mariquita, on the Magdalena river.

Road systems enabled Antioquia to extend its dominion as far as Ambalema, in Tolima, and Palmira, in Valle del Cauca, during the coffee boom era. And money generated by the coffee business would later make possible the emergence of industrial cities.

The *bandeja paisa* (the *Antioqueño* likes to be known as *paisa,* an apocope for *paisano,* meaning fellow countryman) reflects the local people's history and ideology: this dish includes red beans, rice, minced beef, pork cracklings, *patacones* (fried plantain slices) and a fried egg. It is peasant fare with the tardy nineteenth-century addition of rice. The wise combination (rice speeds up the absorption of bean protein) is served in lavish

Coffee-drying, Armenia, Quindío

proportions, as the *campesino* eats his main meal late in the day, after returning from the fields where he has only taken along a jug of *guarapo* (a fermented sugarcane beverage), a few *arepas* and a strip of jerked beef. It is not a refined dish, something which would mean a grave sin according to rural Catholic standards.

A workday in the coffee zone begins at the crack of dawn, with a small cup of black coffee, with or without sugar. Breakfast is being prepared in the kitchen. *Arepas* are being warmed over the fire, water boiled for *agua de panela* or hot chocolate. There is fresh cheese on the table, and an egg for whoever wishes. Sooner or later someone will ask for beans left-over from dinner. This depends more on appetite than on habit. If the peasant has not taken along "a little something" and he is close to home, he will return before noon for a light refreshment: cassava, *arracacha, patacones,* a piece of meat and fruit juice. In the city the rhythm

Arepas de maíz *and* Arepas de choclo

The making and selling of empanadas, *Medellín, Antioquia*

changes. Breakfast and the main meal are taken at home according to tradition. The "little something" brought to work can be a *chorizo,* Spanish-style pork sausage spiced with garlic, a plate of *empanadas* doused in *ají* sauce, cassava or *arracacha* dumplings. There is a wide variety to choose from.

Rural cuisine was limited by the range of products available, by what the earth produced. The first and most important is corn. Typical dishes are derived from it and native methods of preparation. The grains are removed by vigorous pounding in a wooden mortar, which still can be seen in peasant homes, and used in a thousand ways, but the *arepa* and *mazamorra* (boiled grains served with milk and grated *panela*) are always a

daily fare. During the Colonial period and the first hundred years of the Republic, potatoes were scarce, but later they were grown in cold lands where mining was replaced by agriculture. One of the classic dishes of the coffee region is based on potatoes: *mondongo,* a tripe and pork stew. Cacao was cultivated, consumed as a hot drink mixed with cornmeal and *panela.* And plantain, which also provided shade to coffee plants.

Corn, beans, pork and plantain… The first impression is of a monotonous diet. But no, inventiveness intervenes, in other words the housewife in the kitchen. Beans are not always smothered in *hogo.* Sometimes squash is added, or maybe pineapple or even a sweet touch of *panela.* On the table one always finds a saucer of fiery *ají* to

Food store, Caldas

bring out hidden flavors, sprinkled with green coriander. A giant bean variety, the *balú* or *chachafruto*, is frequently served, as a *purée* or *confite*. Sweet cassava is a malleable material: baked in hot ashes and mashed into a dough, sometimes mixed with *arracacha*, it acquires a different taste and unusual texture than merely boiled or fried.

At Christmas, the family feast *par excellence*, cornmeal will serve as a base for *natilla*, a dessert sweetened with *panela*, and *buñuelos*, fried balls of dough made with eggs and cheese.

European influence can be detected in some of the flavors and methods for preparing food in Antioquia. After *Independencia*, many European mining engineers arrive and settle in the province. Holton gleefully relates how, invited by one of these

newcomers to the Medellín of 1820, he experienced once again a taste that he had believed lost forever in his memory: orange marmalade prepared in true English fashion.

The rich and vast variety of desserts and preserves typical of the coffee regions are perhaps due to the new immigrants. Their wives mastered the art of preserves, a skill so necessary in countries with seasons, where fresh fruit is only available for a short period.

This was not the case in Colombia, but even in the tropics fruit ripens or abounds at different times. Tradition took root and adapted to the environment. Preserves and sweets were concocted with produce from the coffee zone orchards. It was not until well into the 20th century that refined

Loading sugarcane, Chinchiná, Caldas

Cattle ranch, Pereira, Risaralda

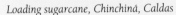

sugar became available for preparing sweets. Sugar loaves obtained in Cartagena at astronomical prices were used, or *panela*, sugarcane sap crystallized by evaporation, widely consumed as most coffee farms had a *trapiche*, the mill where it was processed. The regional drink is *aguardiente*, distilled from sugarcane and flavored with aniseed. It is served in shotglasses and often accompanied by a chaser: green mango or pineapple slices, *uchuvas*, quarters of lemon.

Mistela is a liqueur of Spanish origin, made with *aguardiente* sweetened with fruit, a true household art. In some cases a base of *resacado*, moonshine, was used. Otherwise alcohol was added in small quantities to fruit juice cooked with sugar.

On the map of Colombia, the coffee-producing region does not seem vast. Nonetheless, it is densely populated and highly urbanized. Four cities contend for leadership. Medellín, the capital of Antioquia, main

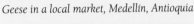

Geese in a local market, Medellín, Antioquia

industrial hub and Colombia's second largest city; Manizales, a financial and coffee research center; and the business towns of Pereira and Armenia. Despite differences, they are driven by a common spirit of tradition… and corn-eating.

The *paisa* is not only a colonizer, he is also an immigrant. His strong commercial tradition has led him to settle down all over the country, bringing his ways with him. There is no road anywhere in Colombia where a typical *fonda Antioqueña* cannot be found, offering his beloved typical dishes.

Mondongo *from Antioquia, a meal in itself, is the local answer to Spain's* callos. *Potatoes, and in some versions roots such as* arracacha, *are* criollo *extrapolations, enhanced by* paisa *inventiveness.*

Mondongo

In Antioqueño *confectioner's jargon, the verb* calar *means cooking fruit so that sugar permeates it without spoiling texture. This technique keeps the fruit whole, while sweetening the pulp all the way to the core, a thrill for the palate.*

Empanada is the name. If its golden crust were not made from corn, one would dismiss
it as just the same old meat pie one finds all over the world. Another difference lies in a
filling of Andean potato and meat seasoned with local herbs.

Empanadas

Tongue in tomato sauce

Among the gifts of Latin America to the European table, and thus to the entire planet's gastronomical culture, beans occupy a place of choice. It would be beyond a Frenchman's imagination to eat roast leg of lamb without white beans. Red beans prepared in paisa fashion is a typical dish which has become daily fare in many parts of the country.

Beans with pig's trotters

Arequipe, *a sweet with countless "secret" recipes, is another legacy from Spain. The large pans where it is prepared, the stirring instrument and the addition of varying ingredients determine the final white, caramel or dark color, and the degree of stickiness with which it adheres to the spoon.*

Arequipe

Coffee

Café

The history of coffee in Colombia would be a book in itself. Indeed, if it is presently grown in several parts of the country, the importance of its production in *Antioquia la Grande* (now divided into the provinces of Antioquia, Caldas, Risaralda and Quindío) cements social and family ties of old and extends beyond the strictly economic. Throughout Antioquia the work day began with *tragos: aguapanela* and coffee. Today the small demitasse of black coffee, known as *tinto*, is the universal fuel for conversation, whatever its nature: politics, finance, religion, sports, business deals, marriage proposals. Anything becomes the pretext to sip a cup of good coffee several times a day: *tinto* is synonym with a good chat.

Natilla

2 liters (8 cups/ 64 oz) of milk
1 lb (500 g) of panela
2 corn starch
2 tablespoons butter
4 sticks cinnamon
1 tablespoon ground cinnamon
1 fresh coconut, grated (optional)

In a large copper pot, boil one liter of milk with the *panela* until the latter melts. With a wooden spoon, remove foam from the surface.
❧ Dissolve the cornstarch in the second liter of milk, and add slowly to the other hot mixture, stirring constantly for 20 minutes until curdling.
❧ Add the butter, the cinnamon and cook over medium heat for ten minutes. Taste to check that the flavor of starch has been eliminated.
❧ If desired, add coconut.
❧ Pour into a dry mold and allow to cool. Sprinkle with ground cinnamon.

Buñuelos

1 lb (500 g) of salty white cheese, grated
1/2 cup cornstarch
1 teaspoon baking powder
2 eggs
oil

Mix all the ingredients together until obtaining a smooth dough. If the mixture seems too dry add a little milk.
❧ Roll the mixture into balls and fry in not overly hot oil in batches of six, until the *buñuelos* fluff up and rise. This should take about five minutes, then turn on the heat until golden.
❧ Remove and drain on absorbent paper.
❧ It is very important to allow the oil to cool a little between batches.

Fruit juices

Jugos de frutas

8 portions

Tangerine

Squeeze 24 tangerines, strain and blend the juice with half-a-liter of water. Add sugar to taste. Serve cold.

Lime

Squeeze eight limes, strain and blend the juice with half-a-liter of water, the peel of one lime, sugar to taste and three ice cubes. Serve immediately.

Blackberry

Blend 500 g of cleaned blackberries, strain, add one liter of water and sugar to taste. Blend again and serve cold.

Orange

Squeeze eight oranges, strain and blend the juice with half-a-liter of water, sugar to taste, and three ice cubes.

Arepa de choclo

10 sweet ears of corn

Remove the grains from the ears of corn and grind into a smooth paste.
❧ Roll into balls and flatten with the palms of your hands, using a damp cloth if desired.
❧ Place on a grill and roast over a low flame, turning the arepas over to cook on both sides.
❧ In the middle of the process, one can slit them open and insert slices of white cheese, replace them on the grill for two minutes or until the cheese melts.

Arepa de maíz

1 kilo of whole corn

Soak the white or yellow corn in water with lye for 24 hours.
❧ Drain and wash well. Scrub to remove husks and impurities.

❧ Cook in fresh water to cover for one-and-a-half hours.
❧ When the corn is soft, remove, drain, grind the grains and knead into a dough.
❧ Shape flat or round arepas and place on a grill over medium heat. Turn over to toast on both sides.

Alfandoque

*I*n Antioquia, *sobremesa* means the same thing as *postre,* dessert. *Alfandoque* is a typical *paisa* sweet, which sprang from children's frolics during Sunday labor in northeastern Antioquia's sugarcane mills. Actually, the *trapiches* resorted on a daily basis to child labor in order to transform low-value *panela negra* into a more saleable product. Thus, children of all ages crush sugarcane, grate coconuts, grease tins and boil molasses, that they stretch, when cooler but still malleable, in spirals around a stick. Three hours of this job guarantee production of 50 *alfandoques* with only two bricks of *panela.* Today, despite their painstaking elaboration, *alfandoques* are still sold in roadside stands, inevitable stops on the traditional "Sunday gastronomical tour" of *paisa* families seeking *sobremesa* to top off the following week's meals.

Chorizos and morcillas

*I*f indeed Spaniards introduced the pig in the Americas, and henceforth all its manners of preparation, *criollos* had their say in its seasoning. For example, the *morcilla paisa* stuffing of blood and rice is blessed with the inimitable tang of a native sprig, *poleo* (pennyroyal). Whereas in Spain there are at least a dozen kinds, local *chorizo* only varies in the proportions of cumin, bacon, green onion, annatto, leg of pork, garlic, *ajíes,* coriander, oregano, salt and pepper. If Spanish *morcillas* and *chorizos* prove different depending on the province of origin, the same goes for *Antioqueño* equivalents, distinct in each valley.

Mondongo

8 portions

4 lb (2 kg) clean beef tripe
1 lb (500 g) pork
3 chorizos, *cut in slices*
1 cup hogao *(see page 142)*
10 cups (8 fl oz/2.5 l) water
4 cups basic broth *(see page 81)*
cumin, pepper, saffron and salt to taste
2 lb (1 kg) potatoes, diced
1 tablespoon coriander, chopped

*C*ook the tripe in water, for one hour in a pressure cooker or three hours in an ordinary pot, until achieving the desired texture. Throw away the water.
❧ Dice the tripe and pork in small cubes, add the *chorizos* and marinate them in the *hogao* for two hours.
❧ In the ten cups of water and the four cups of basic broth, cook the tripe, the pork and the *chorizos* with the cumin, pepper, saffron and salt. Simmer for one hour over medium heat.
❧ Add the potatoes and cook for 30 more minutes until soft.
❧ Add coriander before serving.

Baked bananas

Bananos calados

8 portions

8 tablespoons (4 oz/125g) butter
1 tablespoon lime peel gratings
2 tablespoons lime juice
3 tablespooons sugar
8 bananas

*P*reheat the oven to 200°F.
❧ In an ovenproof dish, put the butter, the lime peel gratings, the lime juice and the sugar. Place in the oven for two minutes, or until the butter melts. Stir well.
❧ Remove the dish and raise oven temperature to 400°F.
❧ Peel the bananas, coat with the butter mixture and place in the oven for 20 minutes.
❧ Remove the bananas from the oven and baste again with the butter mixture. Replace in the oven for an additional ten minutes, until golden.
❧ Serve piping hot.

Empanadas

*F*or the filling:

1 lb (500 g) of beef shank
cumin and salt to taste
1 lb (500 g) potatoes
4 tablespoons oil
1/2 cup hogao (see page 142)

*C*ook the meat in two cups of water with salt and cumin according to taste for one-and-a-half hours.
❧ At the same time, cook the unpeeled potatoes in water with a little salt for 30 minutes. Remove skin and dice.
❧ Cut the meat into small pieces and sauté in oil. Add the potatoes and the hogao, stir well.

*F*or the dough:

1 lb (500 g) of threshed corn
2 tablespoons of cassava starch
2 tablespoons of grated panela
1 tablespoon salt
oil

*C*ook the corn in sufficient water during one-and-a-half hours.

❧ Drain the corn, grind it and mix with the cassava starch, the *panela*, and the salt. Blend together well.
❧ Knead the dough into small balls. Flatten them with your fingers on a damp dishcloth, place a spoonful of filling in the center of each round, fold the cloth over along the middle and seal the *empanada* by squeezing the edges together with your fingers, thus forming a half-moon.
❧ Fry by batches, in abundant, very hot oil until golden. Remove and place on absorbent paper.
❧ Serve piping hot with *ají* sauce and limes.

Fried arepa soup

Sopa de arepa frita

8 portions

5 cups (40 oz/1.25 ml) basic broth (see
  page 81)
5 cups (40 fl oz/) water
1 lb potatoes, peeled and diced
1 cup hogao (see page 142)
salt, pepper and cumin to taste
3 eggs
1 tablespoon cornstarch
6 stale arepas, cut into squares
oil
2 tablespoons coriander, finely chopped

𝒞ook the potatoes in the five cups of
water and the broth with the *hogao*,
cumin, salt and pepper, for 20 minutes,
until the potatoes are soft.
❧ Beat the eggs with the cornstarch and
a pinch of salt. Dip the stale *arepas* in
the mix, than fry in hot oil until golden.
Add them to the boiling broth.
❧ Add the coriander before serving.

Tongue in tomato sauce

Lengua en salsa de tomate

8 portions

1 beef tongue (3 lb/1.5 kg)
1 cup hogao (see page 142)
1 1/2 (1.125 ml) bottles of beer
3 bay laurel leaves
1 tablespoon thyme
salt and pepper to taste
10 large, ripe tomatoes
3 tablespoons (1 1/2 oz/ 45 g) butter
1 teaspoon sugar
1/2 teaspoon black pepper
salt to taste

𝒫ound the tongue a little, wash it
and simmer it in a little water with salt
for 15 minutes. Throw away the water
and skin the tongue.
❧ Cook the tongue covered in water,
adding the *hogao,* the beer, the bay
laurel leaves, the thyme, the salt and
pepper. In a pressure cooker this
should take one hour, in an ordinary
pot three hours.
❧ Remove the tongue and slice. Reserve
the broth.

❧ Place the tomatoes in boiling water
for two minutes, peel, seed and lightly
mash them.
❧ Melt the butter over medium heat,
add the tomatoes, the sugar, a few more
laurel leaves, black pepper and fry for
15 minutes.
❧ Add one-and-a-half cups of the broth
the tongue was cooked in and salt to
taste, stir occasionally until the sauce
thickens.
❧ Heat the tongue in this sauce for 15
minutes before serving.

Patacones

$\mathcal{N}$egro manpower, imported by Spaniards to replace the rapidly-dwindling number of Indians enslaved in the mines, brought along many new culinary elements (not to mention the women's legendary skill with spices), among which plantain. In a land so rich in gold, small wonder that a nugget acquires the same colloquial name as a Spanish coin: *duro* or *patacón*. And likewise, by analogy, a golden slice of fried green plantain. Whatever the etymology may be of such a succulent and inspired preparation, in contemporary *Antioqueño* gastronomy, not only is the *patacón* a perennial fixture in the typical plate of red beans, but also a snack in its own right, eaten at all times of day with cracklings, avocado, *ají, hogao*, shredded beef… Undoubtedly, and without exaggeration, the *patacón* is gold made sustenance.

Beans with pig's trotters

Fríjoles con pezuña

8 portions

2 lb (1 kg) of large red beans
14 cups (112 fl oz/3.5 l) of water
1 1/2 cups hogao
1 1/2 lb (750 g) of bacon or pig's trotters
1 carrot
2 green plantains
salt and cumin to taste

$\mathcal{W}$ash the beans well and leave them to soak overnight.
❧ Cook the beans in the water they soaked in, adding the *hogao,* the bacon or pig's trotters, the grated carrot, the green plantains shredded by hand, the salt and the cumin, for about 45 minutes in a pressure cooker or three hours in an ordinary pot over medium heat, until tender.
❧ Uncover the pot, and allow to simmer over low heat until reaching the desired consistency. Stir frequently.
❧ Remove the bacon or pig's trotters before serving.
❧ More *hogao* can be added upon serving.

❧ If desired, slices of ripe plantain can be added at the beginning, to impart a light sweetness to the beans.

Hogao

2 lb (1kg) of red tomatoes, finely chopped
6 stalks green onions, finely chopped
4 tablespoons oil.
salt and saffron, to taste

$\mathcal{S}$auté the tomatoes and the onions in oil, stir until achieving a smooth sauce. Add salt, cumin and saffron.

Arequipe

8 cups (64 oz/2 l) of milk
2 lb (1 kg) sugar
1 pinch salt
1/2 teaspoon bicarbonate of soda
1 stick cinnamon

*P*ut all the ingredients together in a large pot, preferably copper. Cook high for 20 minutes without stirring, until the mixture thickens a bit.
❧ Lower the heat and stir with a wooden spoon for 30 minutes.
❧ When the bottom of the pot becomes visible, remove from the fire, place in another vessel and allow to cool.

Leg of pork
Pernil de cerdo

8 portions

one 6 lb (3 kg) leg of pork
3 tablespoons salt
1 tablespoon ground pepper
1 teaspoon black pepper
6 cloves
6 garlic cloves
2 onions, halved
2 celery stalks cut in pieces
2 bay laurel leaves
1 bottle of beer

*T*o prepare the marinade for the leg of pork, on the day before blend all the ingredients in beer, and coat the meat with the mixture. Pierce holes in the leg with a spit for better absorption.
❧ Put the leg of pork in a pan and keep in a cool place, turning it over frequently.
❧ Place in an oven preheated to 250°F for three hours. After an hour-and-a-half turn the leg over to brown on both sides.
❧ This dish can be accompanied by *criollo* potatoes, placed in the oven 30 minutes before the leg of pork is ready.

Blackberry mistela
Mistela de mora

1 lb (500 g) of sugar syrup
6 cup (48 oz/1.5 l) aguardiente
2 lb (1 kg) ripe blackberries, cleaned

*P*ut all the ingredients in a glass jar and allow to repose for at least two months.
❧ Add a bit of fresh water if desired to dilute strength.
❧ Strain and bottle.

Following page: Chicha

Cundinamarca
and Boyacá Altiplano

The Eastern Cordillera, the most recent geologically, being a crease from the tertiary period, harbors in its center the Cundinamarca and Boyacá altiplano, formed by plateaus and valleys located between 2,600 and 2,800 meters above sea level.

With rich soils ideal for agriculture, the vast altiplano has been the habitat of human groups for thousand of years B.C. When the European conquerors arrived, the zone was inhabited by various indigenous cultures of the Muisca branch, dominated by the Chibcha.

Selling geese in Sogamoso, Boyacá

The temperature varies between 12 and 18 degrees centigrade. There are no seasons, but two rainy and two dry periods during the year, referred to as winter and summer. The land includes microclimates with great differences in temperature and humidity, and therefore offers the possibility of diversified agriculture.

It was in the altiplano region, which became the administrative and road network center during the Colonial period (from the 17th to 19th century), that wheat, cereal and fruit brought by the immigrants became best adapted. The road from Quito to Caracas passed through Santa Fe, where the main events of the Colonial era inevitably took place.

After Santa Fe, in importance came Tunja, a city of public officials, Villa de Leyva and Oiba, on the way to the province of Socorro, which in the 17th century became the territory's richest trade and craft center.

Since there were no important gold deposits in the cordillera (the precious metal worked by the Chibchas being the product of barter), the natives were condemned to forced farm labor and confined to "Indian villages" established along roads close to their place of slavery. The *encomiendas* were big expanses of land granted as royal titles by the Crown, the token of esteem and gratitude for services rendered.

The inhabitants of the "Indian villages", under the command of an overseer and the moral vigilance of a missionary, had to strive for their livelihood working on loaned land. Nearby, the "white" village, actually populated by *mestizos,* was

Ploughland with oxen, Pantano de Vargas, Boyacá

Sumapaz region, Cundinamarca

built around a church located in the central plaza. If, in this instance, the Indians did not suffer from privations and overwork, as those condemned to the mines, they died of contagious diseases for which they had no defence: measles, chickenpox, smallpox, typhus and leprosy. Two centuries after the conquest began, only about one fifth of the original native population remains on the entire territory.

The Spaniards take only a few Negro slaves to the altiplano, as servants rather than laborers, and women rather than men. Laws banning intercourse between natives and whites are lax, and crossbreeding occurs at an early stage.

In terms of culinary history, the contribution of other ethnic groups proved negligible, and food staples remained indigenous: corn, potatoes, beans, roots, to which little by little Spanish imports were added: onions, garlic, chickpeas, oats, barley.

Society was organized on a self-sufficient basis. Consequently, markets were small, and those offering goods and products from other climates

were the privilege of people with the means to acquire them: namely, a few well-to-do heirs and public officials on the make.

The variety of flavors, the difference of textures, the tentative search for a balanced diet depends on the manner food is prepared. With corn, the Indians know how to produce anything from a fermented beverage, *chicha,* to a biscuit, and a wide palette of soups and recipes to avoid monotony. The technique of shelling corn with lye, in the form of ash, changes its taste and enriches its mineral content. The use of different varieties, the grinding methods, the incorporation or rejection of husks, the way it is refined, sifted and crushed with a stone, make corn a versatile and enriching element. Corn fermented during three days before grinding, to obtain a sour starch, confers an inimitable flavor to bakery.

Contrary to what happened in the rest of the country, lands on the altiplano are taken over rather than colonized. Pork is not as essential a food as it is for miners. Chicken replaces it, perhaps because pigs are more difficult to feed than in warmer climates, where corn grows, harvested twice a year, and plantains and cassava to fatten them.

The expanses of land lend themselves more to cattle raising. Until the late 17th century, slaughtering a cow was an economic crime. The milk trade is based on exchange. Pasture lands are meager, and their distance from markets makes the animal lose so much weight that its sale proves unprofitable. Better to butcher the animal, preserve its meat with the plentiful local salt and sell it to travellers on their way to Socorro, Cúcuta and Venezuela. The government uses it to feed the guards, and hauls it over the road from Vélez to the Magdalena river to sell to boatmen and passengers on their way to the Caribbean.

In the 18th century, forced labor on lands of the *encomendero* has been replaced by payment, to the heir of the entailed estate, of rent in work and a share in harvests. Productive lands belong to the white man. Only a few Indians work on their own lands, poor soils in the boondocks of the *páramos*. The majority of *mestizos*, who have no right to inherit, become day laborers, and only a handful craftsmen or traders.

Except in the larger towns, there are no organized markets, and trading is limited. Communities have to be self-supporting, and if there is a surplus for exchange, only indispensable items are acquired, such as salt and brown sugar. It seems to be a fact that local Indian food was cooked or roasted, never fried. Anyway, on the altiplano,

Lake Iguaque on the páramo *of the same name, Boyacá*

Near Lake Tota, Boyacá

no oleaginous plants were grown, neither was fat extracted from any substance. Fried dishes were a newcomers' contribution. But as pigs, the source of lard, were scarce, boiled food remained the rule.

If any ingredients of Spanish cuisine were missing, they were replaced by *cubio, arracacha,* cassava, *ahuyama, vitoria, ají,* and in warmer valleys, *cidrayota.* From 1780 onwards, the altiplano becomes the route of bread. The big wheat fields and mills lie in the zone of Villa de Leyva and Samacá. Flour goes to Socorro and surplus wheat to the mills of Santa Fe and Tunja. But on stops along the road, muleteers and travellers, instead of white wheat bread, persist in eating *almojábanas, chicheros, garullas,* breads and biscuits made with cornmeal. But how does the Arab word *almojábana*

make its mysterious appearance? Indeed, why *almojábana*? The word comes from the Arabic *mojabena,* a flour tart made with cheese and eggs, butter and sugar fried together, whereas the altiplano *almojábana* is made with cornmeal and cheese.

Another *campesino* dish has an Arabian touch: *indios.* Cabbage instead of vine leaves, stuffed with corn dough instead of rice. A mere coincidence, some will say. But why is the altiplano *morcilla* seasoned with pennyroyal, a variety of mint? Would it be a distant echo of the influence of Arab culture on Iberian peninsula cuisine? One thing we can be sure of is that here we have another example of *criollización.* The food could be justly qualified as rustic. Such an adjective suggests, maybe

mistakenly, an insipid and unimaginative taste. And sure enough, this cuisine is far from sophisticated, and its repertoire of spices doesn't extend further than what the local garden can provide. Maybe this is precisely what retains the delicacy of calabash flowers added to eggs fried in butter. Nobody can deny the nutty flavor of *ibia* cooked with a little salt.

It is unfair to say that altiplano fare is monotonous. Genuine *campesino* food, served in the countryside true to tradition, compensates with a varied starch content for the absence of proteins necessary to restore depleted energies. Traditionally it is low in fat, and soups play an important part in fighting off the cold temperatures reigning in the highlands and humid zones.

A potato broth with a chunk of beef or a *changua* replaced morning hot chocolate in many *haciendas*. *Mazamorra* is a meat and vegetable soup, unique in its kind, sometimes eaten with bread. And if the wind is blowing hard, a couple of spoonfuls of *ají* will stave off the cold. *Cuchucos* of barley, wheat or corn also include meat and vegetables. These are hearty dishes which do not require elaborate preparation.

The potato, in countless shapes and colors, occupies the place held by corn in Antioquia. And Colombia offers a great variety indeed, each one conferring a specific quality to each dish. The *sabanera* is ideal for frying, the *paramuna* for roasts and broths, the *criolla* for thick soups, the *pastusa* for *purées* and soups and the *tocarreña* for baking. Some are rich in starches, others have a high carbohydrate content. Some soups, *ajiaco* for example, require three different varieties to obtain the desired texture and flavor.

In the Sabana de Bogotá, ever since pre-Columbian times, salt was extracted from the Zipaquirá mines. This abundance explains one of the traditional recipes of the region: the *papa salada* (salted potato), cooked in brine until the water evaporates and the tuber is coated by a white shell

Campesinos from Tenza, Boyacá

Onion fields near Tota, Boyacá

Market in Nemocón, Cundinamarca

which crumbles like a sandcastle at the slightest touch.

The region has undergone swift change since the 19th century. The vast latifundia where fractioned into still sizeable *haciendas,* in turn often subdivided again by inheritance laws into parcels of land rarely over a hundred hectares. The same happened in the *páramo* highlands, the poor soils of which have always been tilled by Indians and their descendants.

Mechanization of agriculture and industrialization of cattle ranches forced many peasants to look for work elsewhere. These factors, along with others of a political nature, caused a considerable exodus towards the newly-colonized territories, the growing cities and the wooded and steep mountain slopes of warm lands, where *Boyacenses* cultivated their own plots or became peons. Later on, they pioneered as far as the Orinoco plains and the Amazon jungle. Another important migration took place when *hacienda*

owners and their families moved to Bogotá, where they found a better education for their children, greater comfort and a more interesting social life. The *hacendados* left administrators in charge, and kept, as the popular saying goes, one foot in the province and the other in the city.

This class substantially contributed to the transfer and strengthening of culinary customs, ingredients and processes which today form an established part of regional tradition. Sometimes such changes occur with the arrival of new products, as in the case of trout introduced in Lake Tota over thirty years ago.

The cattle raising boom, spurred by the importation of better grazing grass, breeding stock and technology, proved an undeniable influence on regional diet. Since the fifties, even the most modest farmer keeps a cow, sells its milk or makes butter and fresh cheese. *Cuajada* and country cheese appeared in markets and homes throughout the country, and became everyday culinary ingredients.

Harvesting barley, Cundinamarca

Campesina *shelling corn, Tuta, Boyacá*

Making cheese, Ubaté, Cundinamarca

Fruit stall, Anapoima, Cundinamarca

Cheese was used with *hogo* to cover *papas chorriadas* or *cocido.* Mixed with cornmeal and butter, it improved the flavor of *indios* and *cuajadas en panela,* one of the many delicacies common to Bogotá and altiplano.

Balzac's description of his birthplace's country food can be applied universally: "The purpose of the patient task of those who spend hours of their lives in front of a stove, submerged in a cloud of fragrant fumes emanating from pots where food is prepared to conclude a day's work, is to lovingly achieve, with whatever Providence has granted, a delight for the palate which will soothe the day's sorrows".

Postre de natas, *made with skins skimmed from boiling milk, is undoubtedly of Spanish origin, as seems to indicate the existence of a highly similar Mexican sweet, chongos zamoranos,* except that the latter is prepared with goat instead of cow milk.

Curd with panela and curd with panela syrup

Chicha

The drink nowadays known as *chicha* is only a weak ersatz of the original liquid, which was sold until the beginning of this century in *chicherías* or *pulperías* throughout Bogotá and its surroundings. *Doctor* Jorge Bejarano, minister of health at the time, went down in history as the scourge of *chicha* and its *tienda* outlets, which represented an essential part of popular altiplano culture, by erradicating them completely. Today, *chicha* is prepared differently. Saliva, secreted by old Indian women endlessly masticating, so fundamental a catalyst in the original formula throughout the Andes, is replaced by honey. In other words, ground corn is mixed with a little honey and water, and kept in an earthenware jar for two weeks to ferment, a process often boosted by a piece of putrescent meat or chicken. Later, more water is added, in order to obtain a smooth mush. The resulting substance is rolled into balls, which are reverted to the earthenware pots, previously coated in a layer of ferns.

The pots are filled with water, sealed and heated over a low fire for 12 hours, before reposing in a cool and dark place for ten days, with the daily addition of a little honey. The end product is a refreshing and unquestionably intoxicating drink.

Salted potatoes

Papa salada

4 lb (2 kg) potatoes
1/4 lb (100 g) of salt

Wash and clean the potatoes, and leave unpeeled.

❧ Cook in plenty water for 30 minutes, a time average which varies depending on the type of potato.

❧ When the potatoes are ready, remove most of the water, leaving only enough at the bottom to produce steam during a few minutes, a depth of approximately three centimeters.

❧ Sprinkle the potatoes with salt, cover the pot, and cook high for five minutes more. Take off the lid and remove from the stove.

Wheat cuchuco with pig's backbone

Cuchuco de trigo con espinazo

8 portions

10 cups (80 fl oz/2.5 l) of water
2 lb (1 kg) pig's backbone
1/2 lb (250 g) wheat cuchuco
4 green onion stalks
4 garlic cloves, chopped
4 cups (32 oz/1l) basic broth (see page 81)
1/2 lb (250 g) sabanero potatoes, peeled and diced
1/2 lb (250 g) of fresh green peas
1/4 lb (125 g) of broad beans
1 lb (500 g) of small criollo potatoes, unpeeled
6 cabbage leaves, sliced
1 sprig of coriander
salt and pepper to taste

𝒞ook the pig's backbone in ten cups of salted water at high temperature for 45 minutes, with the wheat *cuchuco*, the green onions and the garlic.
❧ Remove the backbone and cut into small segments.

❧ Add the basic broth, the *sabanero* potatoes, the peas, and the broad beans. Let simmer over medium heat for 20 minutes.
❧ Add the *criollo* potatoes, the cabbage leaves, the coriander, salt and pepper and the backbone segments.
❧ Cover and cook low for another 15 minutes.

Envueltos de mazorca

6 lb (3 kg) of sweet corn grains
1 lb (500 g) of butter
8 egg yolks
1 lb (500 g) of white cheese, grated
1/2 lb (250 g) of sugar
1 tablespoon salt
1 tablespoon yeast
3 cups (24 fl oz/3/4 l) of milk
20 corn husks

𝒢rind the corn.
❧ Add the melted butter, the egg yolks, the cheese, the sugar, the salt, the yeast and the milk to the ground corn. Knead into an even dough and set aside for one hour.
❧ To make the *envueltos*, place a portion of the dough in the middle of a corn husk, fold backwards and insert the extremities into each other.
❧ Steam over a little water for two hours, with a few corn leaves at the bottom of the pot to avoid sticking.

Curd with panela

Cuajada con panela

6 portions

10 bottles (240 fl oz/7.5 l) of fresh milk
1/2 rennet or curdling tablets
1 panela, grated

*W*arm the milk, adding half a curdling tablet, and allow to sit for two hours.
❧ Squeeze in your hands several times until the buttermilk oozes out. Separate and reserve the buttermilk.
❧ When a uniform mass has solidified, drain for three hours in the appropriate sieve, with weights on top in order to extract the last drop of buttermilk.
❧ Cut into portions and cook for three minutes in the buttermilk.
❧ Place the portions in a mold, sprinkle with the grated *panela* and put in the oven preheated to 400°F for ten minutes, until the *panela* melts.
❧ Serve immediately.
❧ The portions of *cuajada* can also be served with cold *panela* syrup.

Panela syrup

Melado de panela

1 panela loaf
2 cups (16 fl oz/1/2 l) water
10 drops lemon juice

*M*elt the *panela* in water, at high temperature.
❧ Once the *panela* is dissolved, simmer over low fire until obtaining the desired consistency.
❧ Before the liquid cools, add drops of lemon to avoid crystallizing.

Postre de natas

8 portions

12 cups (96 fl oz/3 l) of milk
1 lb (500 g) of sugar
2 egg yolks
2 oz (50 g) of raisins

*B*oil the milk, let it set, skim off the skins which have formed on the surface, reserve and repeat the operation until the milk no longer yields skins.
❧ Prepare a syrup with the sugar and a cup of the buttermilk left over from the boil. Add the egg yolks, stirring until fully blended, and then the raisins.
❧ Add the *natas* (milk skins), and cook low for five minutes without stirring.
❧ Remove from the stove. Do not touch until cool.

Following page: Ingredients used for making Mute

Santander and La Guajira

When the traveller reaches the end of the altiplano, he descends into the wide valley of the Suárez river, and discovers a completely different territory. Not only is the topography, of a less placid nature, different, but also the inhabitants.

A fair-haired man is ploughing a field by the road. If it were not for his clothes and sunburnt face, no one would suspect he is a *campesino*. He shows no Indian features, nor does his companion of a darker complexion. Neither does the woman vituperating a stubborn donkey reveal any traces of mulatto or *mestizo* blood. Why this sudden ethnic change?

Before finding an explanation, the traveller leaves behind humid and fertile valleys to enter a zone which is dry but not arid, and discover two cities of evident Spanish origin: Socorro and San Gil. One glance at the churches and the architecture which has survived the cities' random growth suffices to confirm the impression. And the journey continues, over a road which zigzags between

Chicamocha river canyon, Santander

colossal mountains and plunges into the awe-inspiring canyon of the Chicamocha river, its waters shimmering below in deep precipices. The vegetation has changed: no grass, no luxuriant trees, no flowering bushes. A land of goats, full of thorns and cacti.

A description of the northeastern region, so changing and contradictory, would require many pages. After the dry zones, one again ascends the cordillera to the eternal mists of the *páramos,* before going down to tropical Cucutá. Or instead one follows the valley of the Magdalena river, strewn with cotton fields and palm trees, all the way to Valledupar, on the foothills of the Sierra Nevada, or La Guajira, the only desert on the Caribbean.

Here again human physiognomy changes. The traveller will find mulattoes, *zambos,* Negroes and Wayúu Indians, dressed in robes of many dazzling colors. This is a region of many regions. Nonetheless, history, communications and arbitrary solutions to geographical barriers and problems bring them closer to each other, but fall short from achieving unity.

Salt marsh, Manaure, La Guajira

In the 17th century, Socorro was the third most important city in Nueva Granada. Santa Fe was considered the first, being the place of residence for the Viceroy and Archbishop. Second came Cartagena, strategic strongpoint defending and controlling the Caribbean. Socorro enjoyed a privileged status because, for all purposes, the other cities lived off its wealth. It thrived with craftsmen, weavers, hatmakers, embroiderers, traders, farmers and cigar manufacturers. Only gold generated more wealth for the Spanish Crown than the tobacco industry and the taxes imposed on it.

Not the slightest memory is left of the region's Indian cultures. *Visitador* Alvarez writes in 1790: "Of the 30,000 adult Indian males who lived in the region, barely 200 are left. The rest have been annihilated by the secret judgement of God…" Quite an euphemism for epidemics and wars.

For this reason, Indian food and modes of preparation prove of mitigated influence in a region where whites and *mestizos* predominate. Corn, cassava and *arracacha* are basic elements of the local diet, but prepared differently than elsewhere.

The unhospitable hinterland was settled by families of *segundones, criollos* with no right to inherit and forced to seek fortune in mining ventures along the road between Santa Fe and Caracas. Traders and craftsmen followed their steps.

In the history of culture, traders have performed a task other than generating wealth. They are carriers of customs, ideas and items from

Fishermen on Cabo de la Vela, La Guajira

other places, and are more open to change than the peasant, who clings to tradition as tenaciously as to his piece of land. Their role explains changes in cultural behavior, with ensuing culinary repercussions.

In the mid-nineteenth century, a large group of Germans, lured by the success of an earlier immigrant, settled in the area, leaving the unquestionable mark of Teutonic taste on the *sancocho*. The local *sancocho* is a *criollo* version of an Alsatian dish. Just add cassava and plantain, forget the bacon but not the herbs and cloves, and substitute juniper with coriander.

Mute, one of the region's standard dishes, contains unorthodox ingredients. One could define it as a *mondongo* of sorts, as it includes tripe, beef,

pork and *chorizos*. The beef is cooked in vinegared water, a process unheard-of in the rest of the country. Then come corn, vegetables, eggs, chickpeas, noodles and capers, an intricate concoction of rich texture and surprising flavor. Doubtless, the Santander *mute* is a hodgepodge of various culinary traditions.

A hundred years later, English, Dutch and American oil company employees arrived on the scene, bringing their own culinary peculiarities. The oilmen's appetite gave birth to ham and canned-goods industries to supply encampments in the wilderness, and to vegetable gardens which eventually also catered to local markets, where a demand for the novel produce had already been created by the very *criollo* company employees.

This is the only region of Colombia where lamb or *chivo* (goat) is a meat of predilection, once again for historical reasons. In the early eighteenth century, the priest of the parish of Charalá forwards a request to Spain, specifically the diocese of Girón, tentatively inquiring about permission to purchase a herd of goats, "animals which have relieved hunger in other regions, and (…) the people here are poor and needy…"

We do not know who introduced the *chivo* to Colombia, nor which valiant captain dared have it on board. But, almost certainly, the first specimens entered through the Province of Venezuela. In 1789, in La Guajira, two corporals and a lieutenant of the guard perished under a hail of arrows, after pursuing into their territory a horde of Wayúu Indians suspected of having stolen a herd. The violent death of a goat, be it by accident or design, is as serious a matter to the Wayúu as that of a relative. The family has the right of revenge, which means killing the culprit. Nowadays, goat raising is reduced to the arid stretches of La Guajira, and to the barren, eroded valleys and canyons of the Cesar and Santander provinces in northeastern Colombia.

People of the southern province prepare a dish where the main ingredient is goat blood, which gives color to previously-seasoned rice. Another flagrant *criollo* answer to the Spanish *morcilla,* it includes the same essential ingredients, though not in the same quantities, and without the gut casing. Its name, *pepitoria,* is clearly of Spanish origin, but the meaning is different. In Spain, *pepitoria* is a

Near Uribia, La Guajira

Hormigas culonas, *roasted ants*

chicken stew bathed in sauce and without the rice. Northeastern Colombia's *pepitoria* is dry.

In a nutshell, a native dish with an academic name. In Cesar and La Guajira, an equivalent is *friche*, with no rice. Preparation is similar, and lamb *friche* a dish fit for kings. The word *friche* does not appear in any dictionary. It is a local term for a local mixture of the animal's guts, flesh and blood.

The *bocadillo veleño* is a sweet produced on an industrial scale in the Suárez river valley. Colombians call *bocadillo* a solid but sticky fruit paste which comes in individual portions. But the *bocadillo veleño* stands out of the crowd. It is prepared with guavas treated in varying fashion. One layer is bleached, while the other retains the original fruit color. The small cubes of guava paste are wrapped in dried plantain leaves, which convey a delicious aroma, before being packaged in rough cases of light wood. Visitors of the region can see,

Biscuit factory, Bucaramanga, Santander

scattered in fields along the road, the small boards used for this purpose drying in the sun. *Bocadillos* are usually eaten with a slice of fresh cheese low in salt. A less orthodox custom is to stuff baked or fried plantains with guava paste.

A large part of the northeastern region is subject to what cultural geographers call frontier transition. On the border between Colombia and Venezuela, the habits and lifestyles of two nations seem to merge. People speak with a similar accent, and indulge tirelessly in thriving legal and illegal businesses. Political frontiers are arbitrary, and draw artificial lines through regions sharing the same geography and culture.

Immigrants have considerably influenced Venezuelan cuisine. To such an extent that the alleged run-of-the-mill native food resembles more international than typical cuisine. This obviously

Sugarcane mill, Girón, Santander

Market in Riohacha, La Guajira

Food store in Girón, Santander

reflects in cities like Cucutá, in constant contact with the culture and customs of the neighboring country. If the *tamal* is consumed all over Colombia, its local version is closer to the Venezuelan *hallaca,* identical even in size and eaten on the same occasions.

Upon entering this enormous territory with its succession of torrid deserts, humid jungles, warm valleys and mountain peaks shrouded in mist, one is bound to find many distinctive tastes of Colombia.

Callos, tripas or menudo, *all names for tripe, play a leading part in many popular Colombian dishes. The chickpea, a customary ingredient, does not originate from the New World. It was introduced during the Colonial era and became a staple food in the region of Santander perched on the slopes of the Eastern Cordillera.*

Rabbit casserole

Tripe with chickpea

Friche is a name referring to a specific culinary technique rather than a dish. Lamb friche is a meat and gut ragout in gravy made with the animal's blood. Cabrito (kid goat) is served in Santander and La Guajira on special occasions, in varying fashions depending on the region.

Friche

In the country's cold lands, above an altitude of 2,000 meters, people breakfast on a steaming potato broth before setting off for a hard day's work. Ingredients are invariably the same: purple potatoes, a variety which retains a solid consistency, onions and coriander, and if funds allow, ribs to beef the dish up.

Potato broth

Lobster salad

Chocolate

The beverage is a classic example of a "culinary marriage" between two manners of cooking and two cultures. Plainly, native American and Spanish culinary sciences combined to create, with chocolate, a hot drink appreciated and consumed all over the planet. For the indigenous peoples of South America, cacao was just a fruit among many, consumed in its natural state, the mucous membrane around the seed. Spanish inventiveness transformed cacao into a raw material for fine confectionery and a pillar of the food industry. As the story goes, the new-fangled addition to cacao of sugar, cinnamon, vanilla or anise is owed to the nuns of the convent of Guanaca, in Guatemala. However, other historians assert that Colombia was the birthplace of such innovations, since the country, until very recently, had produced the substance in a completely home-made fashion, each *campesino* or urban housewife concocting their own chocolate balls or tablets.

Rice with pepitoria

Arroz con pepitoria

20 portions

goat tripe
3 limes
goat liver, kidneys and heart
8 stalks green onion, chopped
6 garlic cloves, chopped
1 tablespoon of pepper
1/2 teaspoon cumin
salt to taste
1 cup (8 oz/250 ml) oil
2 cups (1 l / 500g) rice
blood of one goat
2 tablespoons of breadcrumbs
5 hard-boiled eggs, finely chopped

Wash the tripe well, inside and out, and rub with lime. Do the same with the heart, liver and kidneys. Cut into pieces.

❧ Cook the lot for one hour, in plenty water.

❧ Remove the meats and mince finely, mix with the onion, the garlic, the pepper, the cumin, the annatto and the salt, and sauté in oil for ten minutes.

❧ Meanwhile, cook the rice in salted water.

❧ With a wooden spoon, chop the clotted blood into pieces. Cook it in a large pot with the minced meat and seasoning for 30 minutes over medium heat. Stir frequently.

❧ Add the rice and stir thoroughly, until hot.

❧ Before serving, garnish with breadcrumbs and chopped hard-boiled eggs.

Mute

8 portions

1/2 lb (250 g) of chickpeas
1/2 lb (250 g) of shelled yellow corn
1/2 lb (250 g) of white corn
1 ox hoof
1 lb (500 g) of beef ribs
1 lb (500 g) of pork
4 green onion stalks
2 onions, peeled and halved
14 cups (112 oz/3.5 ml) of water
1 lb (500 g) of clean tripe
1 pinch of bicarbonate of soda
1/2 lb (250 g) of green beans
1 lb (500 g) of potatoes, diced
salt, pepper and cumin to taste
1/4 lb (125 g) of shredded macaroni
1 eggplant, chopped
1 lb (500 g) of pumpkin, peeled and diced
1 bunch guascas
2 tablespoons of coriander, finely chopped
1/4 (100 g) of capers

Soak the chickpeas and the corn overnight.

❧ If possible, cook the ox hoof the day before in six cups of water and a little salt for 30 minutes, in a pressure cooker.

❧ Remove the ox hoof, cut into small bits and reserve the broth.

❧ Cook the beef ribs and pork with the onions in eight cups of water for one hour, then remove the meats, discard the onions, save the broth and cut the meats into small pieces.

❧ Meanwhile, cook the tripe separately in plenty water, with a pinch of bicarbonate and salt, for 45 minutes in a pressure cooker. Remove and cut into small pieces. Throw out the broth.

❧ Blend the reserved broths and use to cook the corn and the chickpeas for 30 minutes.

❧ Add the beans, the potatoes, salt, pepper and cumin. Simmer for 20 minutes.

❧ Add the macaroni, the eggplant and the pumpkin, cover and cook low for 15 minutes.

❧ Add the ox hoof, the ribs, the pork, the tripe and the *guascas*. Keep on a low fire for ten minutes.

❧ Before serving, garnish with chopped coriander and capers.

Roasted ants

Hormigas culonas

Within the wide palette of regional Colombian cuisine, there are countless dishes of a staggeringly exotic nature, such as *mote de palmito monteriano, relleños de guineo de Ocaña,* or *atollado saperopo huilense.* However, Colombian and foreigners alike wince in disbelief whenever the gastronomic weakness of our fellow countrymen from Santander is mentioned: *hormigas culonas,* literally, roast fat-assed ants. Yet they have become a rare delicacy of international fame. The size of the insect allows for the abdomen and legs to be detached. Once a sufficient quantity of ants has been gathered, they are toasted in a greased *callana* earthenware pot, and stirred carefully to avoid burning. A pinch of salt and… *voilà* ! This delicacy only appears during Holy Week, and always on a sunny day after heavy rains.

Roasted young goat

Cabrito al horno

8 portions

4 lb (2 kg) goat ribs
1 teaspoon saltpetre
1/2 teaspoon cumin
salt to taste
1/2 teaspoon pepper
5 garlic cloves, chopped
2 tablespoons breadcrumbs

Season the ribs with the saltpetre, the cumin and the salt and pepper. Rub with garlic and set aside for one hour.
❧ Cook the ribs in plenty water for 30 minutes in a pressure cooker or one-and-a-half hours in an ordinary pot.
❧ Remove the ribs, set aside, cut into pieces and sprinkle with breadcrumbs.
❧ Place on a greased tin and put into an oven preheated to 350°F for 30 minutes.

Arepa from Santander

Arepa santandereana

2 lb (1 kg) of corn, shelled and cooked
1 cup of cracklings
1 cassava, sliced
salt
1 tablespoon oil

Finely grind the corn, cracklings and cassava.
❧ Add gradually to the dough salt previously dissolved in warm water, and knead for 30 minutes until soft and malleable.
❧ Shape average-sized balls with the dough, place them on a damp dishcloth, and flatten them out with your fingers to desired thickness.
❧ Toast over a low fire, in order not to split, on a greased pan or grill.

Tripe with chickpeas

Callos con garbanzos

2 lb (1 kg) of tripe, cleaned
1 pinch of bicarbonate of soda
1 lb (500 g) of chickpeas
2 tablespoons of lard
2 ripe tomatoes, peeled and diced
4 onions, chopped
4 stalks of green onions, chopped
2 garlic cloves, chopped
1 red pepper, diced
1 teaspoon annatto
salt, pepper and cumin to taste
1 bottle (750 ml) of beer

Soak the chickpeas overnight.
❧ Cook the tripe in plenty water, with the bicarbonate of soda and a little salt for 45 minutes in a pressure cooker.
❧ At the same time, cook separately the chickpeas in salted water for 20 minutes in another pressure cooker.
❧ Cut the tripe in small pieces.
❧ Sauté in lard the tomatoes, the onions, the red pepper, the garlic, the annatto, salt, pepper and cumin.
❧ Add the tripe, the chickpeas, the sauce and, last, the beer. Set aside for 20 minutes.

Rabbit casserole

Cazuela de conejo

8 portions

2 rabbits, cleaned and cut into pieces
1/2 cup (4 oz/125 ml) of bitter orange juice
salt, cumin and pepper to taste
1 tablespoon parsley and coriander, finely
* chopped*
4 tablespoons oil
1 lb (500 g) of carrots, cut lengthwise
4 garlic cloves, chopped
2 tomatoes, peeled and diced
3 bay laurel leaves
1/2 lb (250 g) of onions, diced
1 bottle of beer
1/2 lb (250 g) of green peas
1/2 lb (250 g) of stringbeans

*M*arinate the rabbits overnight in
the orange juice.
❧ Dry the rabbits with paper towels,
season with salt, cumin, pepper and the
chopped parsley and coriander. Set
aside for two hours.
❧ In a casserole, heat the oil and sauté
the pieces of rabbit until lightly golden
all over.

❧ Remove them from the casserole,
pour out the oil, leaving enough to
sauté the onions, garlic and tomatoes
for ten minutes.
❧ Return the rabbit to the casserole and
add the bay laurel leaves, the carrots
and the beer. Stir and add plenty water.
Cover and cook over medium heat for
one hour. Add the peas and the
stringbeans, and cook for another 15
minutes.

Bocadillo veleño

*T*he "flagship" of *Santandereano*
desserts (forget about *cortado de leche de
cabra* or *dulce de grosellas*) is the
eminently traditional *bocadillo veleño*, a
paste made of guava, fruit found in
abundance in the town of Vélez, hence
the name. Yesteryear, it was
manufactured by families of craftsmen,
who also carefully wrapped the product
in dried plantain leaves or corn husks.
Nowadays, *bocadillos* are processed
industrially and marketed in various
forms, in small bars or slices, or filled
with *arequipe*. As happens with other
food products, imitations of the
bocadillo veleño spring up all over the
country... but fail to capture the true
flavor of the original.

Friche

8 portions

1 lb (500 g) of goat offal
salt and pepper to taste
3 lb (1.5 kg) of goat leg, ribs and shoulder
4 limes
1/2 cup (4 oz/125 ml) oil
6 garlic cloves, chopped
3 onions, finely chopped
1 green pepper, diced
2 cups (16 oz/500 ml) of goat blood, mixed
*   with salt*

ut up the offal and sauté in water with a little salt.

❧ Wash the goat meat with lemon, salt and pepper and set aside for 30 minutes. Cut and fry the pieces in hot oil until slightly golden.

❧ Add the offal, the garlic, the onion and the green pepper, sauté for five minutes. Add the blood and simmer gently for 30 minutes, stirring constantly.

Potato broth

Caldo de papa

8 portions

2 lb (1 kg) of potatoes, peeled and cut into
*   slices*
10 cups (80 fl oz/2.5 ml) water
2 tablespoons hogao (see page 142)
salt and pepper to taste
2 tablespoons of coriander, finely chopped

Cook the potatoes in the water during 30 minutes, until soft.

❧ Add the *hogao*, the salt, the pepper and cook another ten minutes.

❧ Before serving add the coriander.

❧ An egg per person may be added if so desired. Cook separately in a bit of broth for three to four minutes, serve carefully in each bowl.

Lobster salad

Ensalada de langosta

8 portions

3 lobsters
salt and pepper to taste
4 tablespoons of lemon juice
4 ripe tomatoes, seeded and diced
2 onions, finely chopped
1 tablespoon vinegar

Cook the lobsters in boiling water with a little salt for three minutes. Reduce to a simmer and cook for an additional 15 minutes.

❧ Throw away the water, cut open the lobster shells, remove the meat in one piece, allow to cool.

❧ Slice the lobster meat and marinate the slices in a mixture of the lemon juice, the tomatoes, the onions, the vinegar and the salt and pepper for 15 minutes.

Following page: Viudo de pescado

Tolima Grande

The narrow Magdalena valley, in central Colombia, was shaped by the turbulent river during the tertiary period. It is flanked by the Central Cordillera, with its active volcanoes, and the Eastern Cordillera, with its craggy peaks. To the south of the valley lies the Andean "knot", where the three cordilleras branch out, and the route to the Amazon. To get there one must cross a range now traversed by roads and descend the Caquetá river, a tributary of the Putumayo, which flows into the Amazon.

Geography and climate in the tropics are always a source of surprises. The valley through which the river passes is dry at first. The foothills of the two cordilleras are humid and, on his way towards the Amazon, the traveller enters a rain forest zone now converted into pasture lands.

Over the last fifty years, the zone has undergone considerable changes. Irrigation systems made possible the cultivation of large expanses of land in the dry valley. The agricultural frontier, which had stabilized on the summits overlooking the Amazon, opened up to the pressure of

Honda, Tolima

colonization. The landscape has suffered radical transformation, and the region has now become a land of farms and cattle ranches.

Before the pre-Columbian era, the region was inhabited by one of the most interesting and little-known civilizations in America: San Agustín, which left colossal stone statues as a mark of its passage on the planet. Its people were talented architects and apparently well versed in astronomy, had an advanced agriculture and grew corn, cassava and cotton. To this day we still do not know what fate this culture met, whether it was annihilated by disease or by war.

Two towns located on the Magadalena river, Honda and Ambalema, and nearby Mariquita, played an important role during the Colonial and Republican eras. Honda, the river port which opened the road to Santa Fe, was an obligatory stop for travellers, a crossroads of sorts. During the 19th century, Ambalema became the country's main tobacco center. From here cigars would be shipped to Bremen, where they competed with Cuban products for a market of exacting amateurs. People

Tabacco plantation near Neiva, Huila

from all over the country flocked to the town. Mariquita was equally important; during the Colonial period as a mining and commercial center, and under the Republic as the capital of the province; in the early 20th century it became a point of transit for the coffee production.

The world of Gran Tolima revolves around an axis formed by Ibagué, Neiva and Florencia, capitals, respectively, of the provinces of Tolima, Huila and Caquetá. But the true common denominator is music, where the local people identify themselves. For them, the biggest national *fiesta* is celebrated once a year on the feast days of San Pedro and San Juan, the patron saints of *bambuco*. At that time every town and village prepares banquets. Wood is cut for the oven that

will roast the *lechona* (suckling pig), stuffed with rice and a mince of its meat and guts, and soused with the juice of bitter oranges to make its hide as crisp as a biscuit. Other delicacies include *insulsos*, made of corn sweetened with *panela* and wrapped in plantain leaves, or *tamales* made of small chunks of pork and chicken and glutinous rice. Into the oven also go *bizcochos de achira* and *pandequesos*.

The plains of Tolima and Huila, and their cultural extension towards the expanses of the Amazon, were not easy to conquer. The region was colonized by two different types of settlers: the *campesino* aspiring to find new lands for his family, and the big agricultural entrepreneur. After the collapse of the tobacco trade, ruined by pests and blights, and the exodus of laborers fleeing the

Fishing in Honda, Tolima

nineteenth-century civil wars, men of enterprise looked for new export products. One of them was quinine. Penetration of the Caquetá jungles starts in the late 19th century. One of the pioneers, Rafael Reyes, who later became president in 1902, searches for and finds quinine, a panacea for malaria, extracted from the bark of a jungle tree. His ambition, however, has a wider scope. Reyes dreams of creating steamship navigation between the Putumayo and the Amazon, in order to export Colombian products to Brazil, and almost succeeds.

In 1854, a young man out of work, José María Cordovez Moure, was a witness to this enterprise. He was not even twenty, barely out of school, and had never touched an axe. Nevertheless, the future author of *Reminiscencias de Santa Fe de Bogotá* joins the group of pioneers: "If work was hard and nights buzzing with millions of aggressive mosquitoes sheer torture, worse still was how we tried to alleviate our sufferings when the time came to sit at the table, a manner of speaking, as we placed plates on our knees, there was no such thing as a table. Food consisted of rice soup seasoned with *panela*, fried green plantains and hot chocolate served in a gourd. Flecks of the cook's dandruff fell in the soup… rice soup of course. Oh no, rice soup again!". Almost a hundred years later, Guillermo Cano, sent by *El Espectador* newspaper to report on the progress of a group of pioneers through the Caquetá jungles, writes: "Here one dances rather than eats. It's the only way to avoid being devoured by insects".

Manufacture of bizcochos de achira, *Neiva, Huila*

Processing tobacco in Campoalegre, Huila

The rice so unappealing to the last century's chronicler remains a basic part of the regional diet, especially today, thanks to irrigation on a large scale. Cassava and plantain, grown on small farms, are next in importance. During recent years, new pasture lands have contributed to increased cattle raising.

Lechona is doubtless the region's most typical dish. Its origins are not clear since Gran Tolima is the only part of the country where pork is stuffed. Even in Spain such a recipe is unusual, except in the north where its is stuffed with a mixture of chestnuts, mushrooms, livers, veal and bilberries. However, the dish has an ancient history. In the 16th century, it was already popular in France, and Gargantua, one of the main characters in the works of Rabelais, often waxes lyrically over the taste of stuffed suckling pig.

If we have not found any mention of *lechona* in travellers'

Selling bizcochos de achira *in Neiva, Huila*

tales and literature before the present century, another *Tolimense* dish, from the Magdalena valley, gets extensive coverage: *viudo de pescado.* In this particular case, no doubts exist as to its Indian origin: ovens not having been invented, pots full of fish were buried in sand on the riverbanks, over which a fire was lit. In order for its flesh not to fall apart during the cooking process, each fish was wrapped in plantain or *bijao* leaves, which have the added virtue of conveying a special aroma. Humboldt, in 1802, savored the dish, prepared by local river people, and it had been famous for a long time before. The name, *viudo de pescado,* seems to have a strange origin. The *bocachico* and the *capaz*, fish used in its preparation, swim upstream twice a year, struggling against the mighty current, in hot pursuit of females which spawn close to the source. This is *subienda* time, a fishing bonanza. Until a few years ago, fish were caught by hand or with traps,

Almojabanas *and cassava bread*

Chicken coops, Neiva, Huila

Pig herds, Neiva, Huila

there was no need for throwing nets. The fishermen thus called *viudos* (widowers) the fish they caught, because the female advance party had almost certainly already suffered the same fate. A diet based on regional products inevitably turns out distinct from others and acquires an exclusive and particular character. *Sancochos* are of indefinite origin, the least sophisticated manner of preparing in one sole pot foodstuffs of varied provenance and quality: meats, vegetables, grains.

One of the regional prides of Tolima is *sancocho de gallina.* Unlike other similar preparations, its is cooked only with the produce of hot plains. Potatoes from the *páramos,* cabbages from the cold lands and carrots from urban gardens are never added. It is made with green plantain, which should be peeled by hand and crushed with a wooden instrument so it doesn't turn black, and cassava, cooked in the broth of a chicken which has pecked around in

Bridge over the Magdalena river, Honda

unrestrained freedom and thus retained in its flesh all the flavors of the land.

And to emphasize this note, tradition commands that it be served with finely-chopped wild coriander. Unintentionally, pioneers of the last century continuously stumble upon novelties. Such as sago palms, which conceal in their enormous stems the finest of flours. Austria and England are the first to buy the product, at high prices, but the boom proves short-lived. The palm takes thirty years to ripen. Another discovery is starch from the *achira* root, with which the local *campesinos* make biscuits of unsurpassed flavor. Europeans have already forgotten about the sago palm. *Achira* will probably wait for another hundred years before a Colombian knight of industry rediscovers and launches it on markets at home and abroad.

When the Spaniards arrived on the American continent, guava trees proliferated all over
the warm lands. Seeds were taken back to Spain, and from there reached as far as India.
The fruit's powerful fragrance, reminiscent of our grandmother's kitchen, has inspired
many exquisite sweets, and even famous books!

Juan Valerio

Guava jelly, paste and stewed rinds

Mistelas *are homemade liqueurs of Spanish origin. Their base is* aguardiente, *to which are added sugar, water if desired, and fruit or aromatic herbs, which impart a subtle flavor to* mistela, *making it an excellent* pousse-café.

Huila roast

Viudo de pescado

8 portions

10 cups (80 fl oz/2.5 ml) of water
2 green onion stalks
4 garlic cloves, chopped
1 big red ají
2 sprigs coriander
salt, pepper and cumin to taste
3 green plantains, cut lengthwise
1 1/2 lb (750 g) of partially peeled
    potatoes, cut lengthwise
1 1/2 lb (750 g) of cassava, peeled and cut
    lengthwise
4 arracachas peeled and cut lengthwise
1 lb (500 g) of pumpkin, unpeeled and cut
    into chunks
8 capaces, cleaned and seasoned with salt
    and pepper
2 cups hogao (see page 142)
2 tablespoons of coriander and green
    onion, finely chopped

Put the water to boil, preferably in a
clay pot, add the onion, the garlic, the
ají, the coriander, the salt, the pepper
and the cumin.
❧ Add the plantains and, in intervals of
ten minutes, the potatoes, the cassava,
the arracacha and the pumpkin.

❧ Add the fish and cook over medium
fire for 20 minutes, with the pot
covered.
❧ Remove the fish and the other
ingredients. Serve them drenched in
hot hogao.
❧ Strain the broth and serve separately,
garnished with the coriander and green
onions.

Achira biscuits with quesillo

Bizcocho de achira con quesillo

The villages of Tolima have made
this succulent pastry into a true home
industry. Actually, the bizcochos of
achira from Altamira and Fortalecillas
are a gastronomical symbol of the
province. Their unique oval shape,
golden color, unmistakable aroma,
crunchy consistency and pleasant flavor
make these biscuits one of the finest
examples of the criollo art of
pastrymaking. The bizcochos are a
combination of cow's milk curd with
the distinctive flour of achira.
Bizcochos de achira are the perfect
complement to hot drinks such as
coffee, hot chocolate or tea, an "angel's
morsel" which can be served with pride
to the world's most sophisticated
gourmets.

Previous page: Stuffed suckling pig in the fashion of Tolima

Tamal tolimense

8 portions

1 lb (500 g) of threshed white corn
1 chicken cut up in medium pieces
salt, cumin and pepper to taste
1 lb (500 g) of fatty bacon
1 lb (500g) of pork ribs
1 bunch of green onions, chopped
3 garlic cloves, chopped
annatto to taste
1/2 lb (250 g) of cooked rice
1/2 lb (250 g) of dried peas, cooked
lightly roasted plantain leaves
lard
1 lb (500 g) of potatoes, peeled and diced
1/2 lb (250 g) of carrots, cut into rounds
3 hard-boiled eggs, sliced
string

*S*oak the corn for three days, changing the water daily. Grind.
❧ Season the chicken with the salt, cumin and pepper.
❧ Simmer the bacon and pork ribs in six cups of water with a little salt for 20 minutes. Remove and reserve the broth.
❧ Mix the ground corn with three cups of the broth. Drain.

❧ In the grease of the bacon sauté the bacon, the onion, the garlic and the annatto for ten minutes.
❧ Add the cooked rice, the peas, and the corn, stirring well and then setting aside for one hour.
❧ For each *tamal* grease one separate plantain leaf. On top of each leaf, place a layer of dough and add bits of the chicken, the bacon, the pork ribs, potatoes, carrots and eggs. Cover with another layer of dough. Fold the plantain leaf bundle-like, tie firmly with string.
❧ Cook in the broth mixed with plenty water for 2 1/2 hours in a covered pot.

Juan Valerio

8 portions

4 green plantains
1 lb (500 g) of bacon
2 stalks of green onion, finely chopped
salt to taste

*P*eel the plantains and bake them in an oven preheated to 300°F for ten minutes. Meanwhile, fry the bacon to a crisp.
❧ Pound the plantains with the onions and the salt, add the hot, crisp bacon and roll the mixture into balls. Serve promptly.

Cassava bread

Pandeyuca

2 lb (1 kg) salty white cheese, grated
1 lb (500 g) of cassava starch
2 egg yolks
4 tablespoons of butter
salt to taste

*M*ix the cheese, the starch, the egg yolks, the butter and the salt. Knead into a smooth dough. Set aside for 30 minutes.
❧ Form the dough into small balls or halfmoon shapes. Place them on a greased tin and put into an oven preheated to 350°F for 20 minutes.

Almojábanas

1 lb (500 g) of shelled corn
3 lb (1.5 kg) of fresh cheese
3 egg yolks
4 oz (125 g) of butter
salt to taste

*S*oak the corn for three days, changing the water daily.
❧ Drain the corn and grind it with the cheese.

❧ Add the egg yolks, the butter and the salt. Knead the mixture until obtaining a smooth and homogeneous dough.
❧ Shape into small balls, place on a tin and put in an oven preheated to 350°F for 20 minutes until golden.

Huila roast

Asado huilense

8 portions

8 lb (4 kg) of boneless pork
2 beers (1500 ml)
1/2 cup (4 oz/125 ml) vinegar
2 tablespoons of bitter orange juice
4 stalks of green onion, chopped
8 garlic cloves, chopped
1 teaspoon of coriander, chopped
1 teaspoon of mint
1 teaspoon of pennyroyal
1 teaspoon of oregano
4 ground bay laurel leaves
1 teaspoon thyme
1/2 teaspoon of grated nutmeg
salt, cumin and pepper to taste

*P*ierce the meat, season it with a mixture of all the ingredients. Set aside to marinate for a minimum of 24 hours.
❧ During this period of time baste frequently, rubbing the mixture thoroughly in.
❧ Place the meat in a clay pot and place in an oven preheated to 250°F for four hours.

Guava rinds

Casquitos de guayaba

8 portions

2 lb (1 kg) ripe guavas
6 cups (48 fl oz/1.5 ml) water
3 lemons
2 lb (1 kg) sugar

Cut the guavas in half, and extract their pulp. Put the rinds in the water with the lemon for one hour. Strain.
❧ With the water and the sugar prepare a very light syrup, cook the rinds over low heat for 20 minutes until obtaining the right consistency.

Guava jelly

Jalea de guayaba

8 portions

2 lb (1 kg) of ripe guavas
2 lb (1kg) sugar
2 lemons

Clean and slice the guavas. Cook in plenty water for 20 minutes.

❧ Remove and strain, extracting all the juice. Reserve the pulp for the following recipe.
❧ Mix the juice, the sugar and the juice of the two lemons and cook over low heat for 35 minutes.
❧ Place in a jar and allow to cool until jelling.

Guava paste

Cernido de guayaba

8 portions

2 lb (1 kg) ripe guavas
3 oranges
2 lb (1 kg) sugar

Mix the pulp left over from preparing guava jelly with the orange juice, add the sugar.
❧ Cook this mixture over a low heat for 40 minutes. Stir with a wooden spoon until the bottom of the pot is visible. Remove from heat and allow to cool.

Marjoram mistela

Mistela de mejorana

1 bunch marjoram and immortelle
1 bottle of aguardiente
5 cups (40 fl oz/1 1/4 ml) water
1 lb (500 g) sugar
1 cinnamon stick
1 tablespoon lemon juice

Put the herbs in the *aguardiente* and set aside for 30 days.
❧ Prepare a light syrup with the water, the sugar, the cinnamon and the lemon juice. Mix with the *aguardiente*.
❧ Keep well covered.

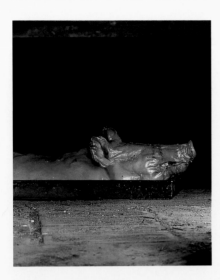

Roasted suckling pig
Lechona tolimense

Lechona tolimense is to this area of the country what beans are to Antioquia, in other words, the symbol of Tolima's cuisine *par excellence*. Its preparation involves a hard day's work, which begins with slaughtering the animal, then making the seasoning and stuffing before roasting in a traditional brick and mud oven. The suckling pig, once slaughtered, is cleaned and gutted, its hide abundantly salted to become crisp. It must be basted with bitter orange juice before being placed in the oven, an operation repeated several times during the roasting process to insure a luscious, glowing auburn color. The stuffing combines onions, peas, potatoes and rice, mixed with meats previously seasoned with cumin, garlic, onion, pepper and salt. Perhaps *lechona tolimense* is not particularly attractive in its final presentation, but its particular, mouth-watering aroma undoubtedly invites to gluttony.

Green beans with ribs
Fríjoles verdes con costilla

8 portions

1 1/2 lb (750 g) of pork ribs, cut into
  small pieces
1 sprig of rosemary
1 sprig of thyme
2 bay laurel leaves
salt and pepper to taste
1 lb (500 g) of green beans
6 cups (48 fl oz/1.5 l) of water
2 cups (16 oz/1/2 l) basic
  broth (see page 81)
oil
2 green onion stalks
2 garlic cloves, chopped
2 tomatoes, peeled and diced

*S*eason the ribs with the rosemary, the thyme, the salt and the pepper. Set aside.
❧ Cook the beans in six cups of water and the two cups of basic broth for 45 minutes, or until they are soft and soupy.

❧ Fry the ribs in a bit of oil until golden, add the onions, the garlic, the tomatoes and a cup of the bean broth, simmer for 15 minutes over low heat.
❧ Mix the beans with the ribs and simmer until achieving the desired consistency.

Following page: ingredients used for making Guarapo

Orinoquia and Amazonia

Although, precisely speaking, this geographical complex goes under two names, because of climatic and therefore biotic differences, there is no clear-cut or determined limit between them. Orinoquia is predominantly formed by grassy plains and scrublands studded with patches of bushy vegetation, *matas de monte* or *bosques de galería* growing along rivers and streams. During winter large stretches are flooded. The waters subside in August and September.

Near the foothills and Arauca and Meta rivers, soars a large rocky formation of igneous origin, the Sierra de Macarena, now declared a national park for its exceptional flora and fauna. In eastern Orinoquia, on the fringes of the Orinoco, we find another formation, impressive masses of rock dating from the secondary period: the *Escudo de Guayana,* rich in minerals, iron, gold and, geologists claim, diamonds. As one progresses southward into the equatorial zone, the trees grow taller. However, the soils are poor, the forest keeps alive thanks to an

Tuparro river rapids, Vichada

transformation. If one cuts the trees and plants, the soil will only yield one harvest, before becoming barren for ever.

In the jungle, many species live together. The tree predominant in low-acid soils often reaches a height of over 30 meters. Below grow ferns, palms of the *bactrix* family, and smaller trees, *yebaros,* their branches full of a constellation of parasites. A botanical compilation proves an arduous task indeed: on one hectare can be found more than 80 plant species, according to the most conservative estimates.

In Orinoquia as in Amazonia, rivers carrying sediments are referred to as "white" rivers and plentiful in animal life. The biggest fish are the *valentón,* which can weigh over fifty kilograms and measure up to three meters, the tiger catfish of similar weight and the scaly *cachama,* delight of gourmets and sportive fishermen for its unique taste.

In the "black" rivers, fish are of lesser size, because the waters are poorer in nutrients. The most abundant reptiles are *Terecay* turtles, the eggs of which are used by natives as a source of food and oil, and *cachirre* or *babilla* crocodiles, presently in danger of extinction. It would be redundant to repeat what the entire world already knows, that the Amazonia-Orinoquia habitat is the planet's richest in bird species. Scientists have identified 47 families, meaning hundreds and hundreds of species and thousands and thousands of subspecies. Few, very few, are edible, be it because of size, scant flesh or taste.

Neither plains nor jungles abound in mammals: there are only few specimens per square kilometer. The most gregarious animals are monkeys known under various names: *titís* (capuchins), *viudas, aulladores* (howling monkeys), *maiceros* and *marimondas.* Also social, as they live in herds, are *cafuches* (wild pigs) and *chigüiros*, the

world's largest rodent, which gather during summer around pools left by the subsiding waters, and the meat of which is highly succulent. This animal is widely consumed in Venezuela: *chigüiro* hams rival with the best pork equivalents.

Until not very long ago, deer abounded, but unchecked hunting has put them on the brink of extinction. The *camerudo* cannot escape into the jungle because of its magnificent set of antlers; the smaller *soche,* which lives in the plains, manages to find refuge in the thickets.

Several different tiger families inhabit the zone; the famous jaguar, which can weigh up to 120 kilos, the smaller puma, and the most beautiful of all, the *tigrillo* or ocelot, prized for its skin. Less persecuted is the wildcat, which has escaped the

Lake Tarapoto, Amazonas

general slaughter. In this enormous region covering over a million square kilometers, today there are only 70,000 Indians. Four hundred years ago, according to chronicles, they were "as numerous as ants" and have populated the region as far back as 6,000 B.C. The bountiful hunting, fishing and picking resources helped them settle. Around 4,000 B.C., a five-century drought almost wiped out wildlife. It was at that time that wild manioc was first cultivated and "cut and burn" agriculture was born. Wild manioc is poisonous if not processed. The process which makes it edible, easily transportable and durable is different in each culture, but roughly similar. The Barasana, according to Christine Hugh Jones, prepare it in the following manner: "…The women peel it with a machete and grate it on boards studded with sharpened quartz tips. The resulting paste is washed, and immediately pressed in the *sebucán*, a cylindrical basket which is hung on a propped fork. The *sebucán* is stretched tight, to squeeze out all the liquid. The gratings are then placed in the sun, and then, when half-dry, in pots, the *budare*, over a fire. The end-product is *casabe*, mixed with water at eating time".

The Indian eats *casabe* with fish, with produce from his garden: pineapple, squash, *chontaduros*, plantains. If he is a hunter he eats it with game, but the Indian considers hunting a difficult task best left to specialists. He hunts out of necessity, eventually using traps for small animals, rodents and sometimes monkeys. In all the riverside

Plains near San Antonio, Casanare

Preparation of ternera a la llanera *near Yopal, Casanare*

gardens, as anthropologist Martin von Hildebrand calls them, the natives also grow food for their animals. Along with medicinal herbs, hallucinogenic lianas and plants such as *yagé*, coca and tobacco, which are consumed during feasts or rituals. These are "foods for thought". With *yagé*, according to Gerard Reichel-Dolmatoff, they claim to be able "to visit the origin of reality: the Milky Way".

In native gardens one always finds some variety of *ají*, ubiquitous in cooking. In Amazonia there is a kind picked in the jungle, smoked, ground and mixed with salt, called *úquitania*. Also grown is *achiote*, which, if indeed used in the kitchen as coloring, fulfills other, more important functions: symbolic face or body-painting in rituals and ceremonies.

Fruits replace spices. They are considered side dishes. The concept of "sauce" or "marinade" does not exist. If a fish is cooked with guava, the idea is not to improve taste but to use

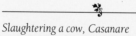

Slaughtering a cow, Casanare

symbols, to establish a harmony between land and water. Settlers in Amazonia and Orinoquia have largely adopted the Indian diet. Game, fish, cassava, plantain and, according to season, turtle eggs, iguana and fruit. They also plant corn. Food is mostly boiled, sometimes roasted. Frying oil is scarce, having to be brought in from the nearest town. Beef or pork is salted and dried, or smoked. To prepare fermented beverages they use corn or *chontaduro* to which pineapple is added, the sugar content of which speeds up the process.

As climatic conditions and rough terrain in the plains are unfavorable to agriculture, extensive cattle raising has been the rule since the 18th century, when the territory began to be colonized. Poor quality of grass is compensated by immensity of pastures. A herd of a hundred heads of cattle requires 500 hectares, and such vast stretches cannot be fenced off. Cowmen identify cattle by their brands.

Ternera a la llanera *and Chitterlings*

 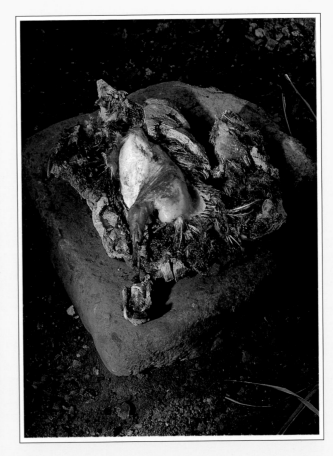

Preparing guinea fowl baked in clay

Driving the herds to market was, until recently, a task which took weeks, if not months. To replenish their energy in regions without agriculture, cowmen had to slaughter animals and eat them as rapidly as possible, wasting none of the meat. Fires performed the double task of roasting meat and keeping tigers away.

Roasting a steer on the plains remains a ritual to this day. The lean meats are rolled in fattier ones, which confer flavor and prevent the lean meats from shrinking and toughening. The meat is brought close to the fire, but not in direct contact with the flames. The result, juicy, and never dry nor burnt, is served on disposable plates: large leaves torn from surrounding trees. Another custom of meat preparation has disappeared. As salt was scarce, meat not immediately consumed was placed, Tartar-style, under the saddle, to be cured by the horse's sweat. A few minutes in the sun were enough to dry it, and *voilà*…

In these plains, where no horizon is visible at night and constellations show the way, or in the darkness of jungles, there is neither room nor time for the leisurely or creative invention of a new dish.

There are no cosy corners. Someone lights the fire. Others slaughter the animal, pick fruits or dig up roots. Soon everyone will be eating, without ceremony. But with the pungent spice of hunger.

Rivers of jungle and plains are teeming with fish, but it is difficult to catch them during the rain and flood season. On the other hand, in summer fish are trapped in pools and puddles, an easy prey. Smoking fish is more a method of conservation than a gastronomical refinement.

Pumpkin Bake

Smoked fish

Guarapo

The Llanos Orientales are a region of intense sun and heavy rains. Its arid climate, in the sun or shade, day or night, winter or summer, creates a permanent state of craving thirst in the inhabitants, mostly cowmen and farmers. Small wonder then that the region offers a wide variety of drinks, the names and ingredients of which deserve gastronomic study: *atol, chicha de arracacha, guarulo, chicha de moriche, carambolo* and *chontaduro* juices, *majule, seje* and *vinete.* Nonetheless, just as in other parts of the country, the Llanos have their own version of the refreshing *guarapo*: shelled and ground corn, in lieu of pineapple or bitter orange, is mixed to the sugarcane juice. A little fresh water is added and the liquid is allowed to ferment for three days or more.

Ternera a la llanera

In the Colombian *Llanos Orientales,* preparing *ternera a la llanera* demands a worthy occasion. Weddings, village *fiestas,* political conventions, rodeo tournaments or just plain binges are events fit for eating what *Llaneros* fondly call *mamona.* A calf about one-year-old is slaughtered, and an expert butcher is required to carve the meat into cuts of different flavor and texture without wasting one morsel of the animal. The most coveted pieces are ribs, topside and fillets, all cut very thinly and seasoned with beer and salt only. The meats, spitted on large, greased sticks forming a circle around the fire (known as *burro*), cook for a long time, as they are not exposed to flames but to glowing embers. The task of preparing *ternera a la llanera* takes an entire day.

Chitterlings

Asaduras

8 portions

1 lb (500 g) of calf liver
1/2 lb (250 g) of hog spleen
1/2 lb (250 g) of lung
1/2 lb (250 g) chunchullo sausage
1/2 lb (250 g) kidneys
1/2 lb (250 g) heart
salt to taste
fatty membrane, to wrap with

Cut the meats up in pieces and spit them in alternating order on long wooden skewers.
❧ Sprinkle with salt, wrap in the fatty membrane and string up tight.
❧ Barbecue with the skewers planted obliquely over live coals, for 50 minutes approximately, turn over occasionally.

Manioc flour

Fariña o mandioca

𝒞assava is a classical Latin American culinary element. However, one must stress that there are two types of cassava: the sweet variety found on markets in the country's central, western and coastal regions, and the wild, poisonous variety, containing hydrocyanic acid, found in the Llanos, Orinoco and Amazon territories, where the inhabitants resort to Indian wisdom to remove the poisonous juices from the root and transform it into edible flour. The flour is called *fariña* or *mandioca,* names of Portuguese origin, and is used to make *casabe* cakes, which serve the same purpose as *arepas* or bread in the rest of the country. Manioc flour is also used in a simple recipe: fry it in a pan with butter and salt until golden, serve hot with soups, meats, or fish… This is called *farofa,* like in neighboring Brazil.

Guinea fowl baked in clay

Gallineta en barro

2 portions

1 fat guinea fowl
1 lemon
2 tablespoons vinegar
1 green onion, finely diced
2 teaspoons thyme
salt and pepper to taste
4 lb (2 kg) clay

𝒦ill and gut the fowl, cut off the head.
❧ Hang it by the feet in a cool spot outdoors for three hours.
❧ Cut off the feet and the wing tips and discard. Prepare a mixture of lemon juice, vinegar, onion, thyme, salt and pepper, and season the bird's inside.
❧ Mix the clay in water until achieving a malleable consistency, coat the bird completely in a two-centimeter-thick layer until forming a ball.
❧ Bury inside hot coals, bake for two hours, turn over every 30 minutes.
❧ Break open the clay ball, feathers should be stuck to the clay fragments, leaving the bird clean.
❧ Accompany with green plantain baked in the same coals.

Pumpkin bake
Capón de auyama

8 portions

1 12 lb (6 kg) auyama pumpkin
2 lb (1 kg) of jerked pork, cut into chunks
2 lb (1 kg) of white cheese, cut in squares
3 cups guiso (see page 50)

Slice off the top of the pumpkin, remove the seeds and clean thoroughly.
❧ Mix the meat, the cheese and the *guiso* and stuff the pumpkin with the mixture
❧ Replace the top and put the pumpkin into an oven preheated to 300°F for one hour.
❧ Cut into portions and use the pumpkin rind segments as dishes.

Smoked fish
Pescado ahumado

In the Amazon, fish are smoked on a wooden armature called *espetón*. This is a square or triangular grill made of green twigs tied with vines to a frame of green wood (to prevent burning).
❧ The *espetón* must be placed a meter over the fire to achieve a gradual smoking process. Timing depends on the size of the fish; small ones take about six hours.
❧ Fish of less than a pound tend to be smoked whole. Larger ones are gutted and scaled.

Baked plantains
Plátanos asados

Peel plantains of the *guineo* variety, or ordinary green ones.
❧ After rubbing in salt, place in the glowing embers of a fire for three hours.

Gastronomic Bibliography

Initial research on the recipes which appear in this book was based on the *GRAN LIBRO DE LA COCINA COLOMBIANA* published by Circulo de Lectores. The books listed below, and chefs through-out the country, were then consulted to enrich and complete the study. All the recipes were carefully kitchen-tested to check accuracy of proportions, cooking time and seasoning.

ARBOLEDA, ANA CECILIA (Editing and production): Aliméntese Bien. Vol I. Undated. Vol ll, 1986.Vol lll, 1987. Bogotá.

FONNEGRA DE SILVA, SOPHIE: Mis mejores recetas. Editorial Kelly. Bogotá, 1943

GARCIA, INES DE y LUCIA DE MARTINEZ: El menu diario. Editorial Andes. Bogotá. Undated.

GOMEZ DE VARGAS, ANA: Gourmet Club, Vol l. Bogotá. Undated.

HERNANADEZ, ELISA: Manual practica de cocina. Vol l y ll. Editores Felix de Bedout e hijos. Medellín, 1969. Eleventh edition.

HOLLMANN, FENITA DE: Minuta del buen comer. Editorial Cromos. Bogotá, 1937.

LLERAS DE OSPINA, ISABEL (Compiler): Secretos de cocina. Editorial ABC. Bogotá, 1948.

OLAYA, CLARA INES: Frutas de America Tropical y Subtropical. Editorial Norma. Bogotá, 1991.

ORDONEZ, ANGELA DE: Cocina Tradicional. Editorial Kelly. Bogotá, 1962.

ORDOÑEZ, CARLOS (Researcher): Gran libro de cocina colombiana. Circulo de Lectores. Bogotá, 1984.

OSPINA DE NAVARRO, SOFIA: La Buena Mesa. Editorial Norma. Bogotá, 1991.

R. DE RESTREPO, ISABEL y EMILIA OLANA MORENO: La cocina, el mesa, y el servicio moderno. Medellín, 1940.

RESTREPO DE CARO, MARIA: Las recetas de mamá. Editorial Presencia. Bogotá, 1977. Second edition.

ROMAN DE ZUREK, TERESITA: Cartagena de Indias en la olla. Ediciones Gamma. Bogotá, 1991. Twenty-first edition.

ROSENBAUM, ETTICA DE (research and editing): El menú diario colombiano. Circulo de Lectores. Bogotá, 1991.

SALAZAR, REGINA DE: Cocina colombiana fácil. Ediciones Triangulo. Medellín.

Index of Photographs

Alphabetical Index
of Recipes